Have I Got a Deal for You!

How to Buy or Lease Any Car Without Getting Run Over

2nd Edition

D1446512

By
Kurt Allen Weiss

CAREER PRESS
3 Tice Road, P.O. Box 687
Franklin Lakes, NJ 07417
1-800-CAREER-1
201-848-0310 (NJ and outside U.S.)
Fax: 201-848-1727

HAVE I GOT A DEAL FOR YOU!
HOW TO BUY OR LEASE ANY CAR WITHOUT GETTING RUN OVER
SECOND EDITION
ISBN 1-56414-301-5, $12.99
Cover design by The Visual Group
Back cover author photo by Judith L. Vick
Printed in the U.S.A. by Book-mart Press

To order this title by mail, please include price as noted above, $2.50 handling per order, and $1.50 for each book ordered. Send to: Career Press, Inc., 3 Tice Road, P.O. Box 687, Franklin Lakes, NJ 07417.

Or call toll-free 1-800-CAREER-1 (NJ and Canada: 201-848-0310) to order using VISA or MasterCard, or for further information on books from Career Press.

Library of Congress Cataloging-in-Publication Data

Weiss, Kurt Allen, 1952-
    Have I got a deal for you!: how to buy or lease any car without getting run over / by Kurt Allen Weiss. -- 2nd ed.
        p.   cm.
    Includes index.
    ISBN 1-56414-301-5 (pbk.)
    1. Automobiles--Purchasing. 2. Automobile leasing and renting. I. Title.
    TL162.W39   1997
    629.222' 0296--dc21   97-21599
                                                            CIP

Acknowledgments

With special thanks and acknowledgments to:

Judy (Judith L. Vick) for all of the time and effort you put into seeing this book completed. Your love, support and faith in me will never be forgotten. Together, we can make a difference!

My mother and stepfather, Lorraine and Bert Johansen. I could have never gotten this far without all of the help and support you gave me. I will always be in your debt, and you both will always be in my heart.

My sister Kim Lauzon, for all your valuable help and suggestions.

My good friend Roy DeVries. Thank you for your faith in me. You know the important part that you played in helping me with this book. My eternal thanks and gratitude.

My publisher and newly found friend, Ron Fry of Career Press. Thank you for giving me the opportunity and means to help so many consumers.

And let me not forget all of the car dealers and salespeople who continue to practice deceptive sales techniques. If it were not for all of you, there would be no purpose to this book.

Contents

Preface

*"If you trust car dealers and car salespeople,
then you don't need to read this book!"*

There are few things in life that we depend on more than our automobiles. There are also few things in life that most of us dislike more than the thought of having to deal with car dealerships and salespeople. It's unfortunate that what should be an exciting and rewarding experience is so often ruined by the deceptive and high pressure selling practices that are still used today by many car dealerships and salespeople.

This book will expose many of the deceptive practices the automobile industry will attempt to use against you. It is also a guide that will show you how to turn the negotiating advantage car dealerships have had for so long back to your side. It will teach you simple, easy-to-use shopping and buying techniques that will enable you to save hundreds, even thousands, of dollars on all your future automotive purchases. But even more importantly, the book is designed to make the process of shopping for, buying and owning an automobile a fun and rewarding experience.

It doesn't matter if you are going to be buying your first or 50th vehicle. It doesn't matter if you buy one vehicle every 10 years or 10 vehicles every year. It doesn't matter if you intend to pay cash, finance or lease. *Have I Got a Deal for You!* has money-, time- and effort-saving tips for everyone!

The deceptive side of the automotive sales industry is struggling to keep one step ahead of consumers, like yourself, who have educated themselves by reading books such as this one. Take what you read here very seriously because, unfortunately, some things never change! As long as there are opportunities for those businesses and individuals who insist on maintaining a less-than-admirable level of ethics, consumers will always have to be prepared to fight back.

"Have I Got a Deal For You!" is your opportunity to fight back. It is your opportunity to level the playing field and come out a winner. And I should know. I have worked within the automotive sales industry for more than 15 years. If there was ever a time that you needed to trust a car salesman, the time is now! I promise I won't let you down.

—Kurt Allen Weiss

What's new in this edition?

In this second edition of the book, many areas have been updated to reflect the changes that have been happening within the automotive sales industry the past few years. Some of the new topics include:

"Shopping on the Internet"
"Special Finance Departments"
"Used Vehicle Leasing"
"Auto Malls" (new and used)
"Lease Contract Disclosure"

These and more are the topics that will make you a more informed consumer and a better shopper.

On a personal note: Since the first edition of this book was published, I have been asked many times, by the media and consumers alike, whether I am still in the automotive sales industry. The answer is a definite yes. Recently, I have been part of a management team for a multifranchise dealership. My responsibilities include helping to educate consumers, specifically in regards to leasing, and improving customer satisfaction and dealer-to-consumer relations. Of course the side benefit to this is that I am always kept up-to-date on the latest developments within the automotive sales industry, enabling me to offer you the most timely information available.

Introduction

Welcome to *Have I Got a Deal for You!* Being referred to as the "Benedict Arnold" of the automotive sales industry has not made me, nor has it left me with, many friends in the car business. But I didn't write this book to make friends. Not within the automotive sales industry anyway. I wrote this book because I believed that it was time that consumers really understood how car dealerships and car salespeople really make their livings, and in turn, cost you money. Sure, there are all sorts of books and publications available today looking to teach you how to shop for and buy cars. So what then makes this book any different? As an "insider," I felt that the majority of these publications fell far short of giving you the tools that *you* want and need to make the best deal on your next automotive purchase. Many of them try to teach you how to become a better negotiator. Is this what you really want to learn? My experience says no. You don't want to learn how to become a shark. You want to learn how to avoid them. Some publications attempt to teach you how to get the "best price" on your next automotive purchase. I can tell you now that after you have read this book, you will never define the "best price" the same way, ever again.

Although many of you may look at this book as purely a reference guide and may read only the chapters that are of interest to you, I strongly suggest that you read the entire book. Part of making the right decision about anything includes knowing the right questions to ask. Many people who read the first edition of this book, have met me or have had the opportunity to attend one of my seminars, told me that it changed the entire way that they perceived the automotive purchase experience. As long as you have gone this far in your quest to become a more educated consumer, why not go just one step further and read the whole thing? Who knows, you too may discover new and enlightening ideas that may change your buying habits forever!

Few consumers leave a car dealership without wondering, "Did I really get the 'best deal,' or was there something else that I should have done or that I should have known to do?" Such questions often leave us feeling unsure about the deal we made. The worst part about these questions is that most consumers will never know the true answers. Much of the automobile sales industry is based on misleading or deceptive sales and advertising practices. This means that you are often unaware of what or how such deceptions have been used against you. In fact, many consumers are sold into believing that they got a good deal, when in fact, they have been taken advantage of. Let's face it. Few of us go home and say, "Guess what, dear? I got ripped off today." A good salesperson will always leave you believing that you got the "best deal."

Other consumers are simply frustrated because they believe they can get more of a discount than the dealer can actually give them. So afraid of being taken advantage of, this kind of consumer often pushes his or her negotiating to a point where the dealer sees no way out but to deceive him or her.

When I first wrote this book, the most important decision I had to make was what approach I would take to helping consumers. Certainly, exposing deceptive and confusing sales techniques needed to be a part of it, but I realized that this alone would not be enough. What could I really offer consumers that would make a difference, without attempting to teach them how to become car salespeople themselves?

Most of us approach winning a game with the idea that we have to be better than our opponent. Maybe you want to beat your friend at tennis, so you take some lessons and practice more often. Unfortunately, when it comes to dealing with automobile salespeople, your opponent is a paid professional, someone who gets to practice his or her craft every day. Regardless of how much time or effort you put in, the best that you can usually hope for is to become an educated rookie who has to go up against a seasoned pro! It sounds a little disheartening, doesn't it? You work hard at preparing to play the game, just to discover that you have little chance of winning. In fact, it's worse than that. Negotiating for a car is a game that few consumers want to play!

All you want is to be able to get a fair deal and not be taken advantage of.

Well, there is a solution—and it's the one on which this book is based. Consumers usually lose the negotiating game because the sales industry has always determined the negotiating rules. Certainly, the ones who determine the rules have already created a distinct advantage for themselves. But who said that you have to play the game the way they want it played? I say, nobody!

It was this line of thinking that finally offered me, and now you, the solution to my original problem: What approach would I take? The key approach to what you are about to read is to provide you with a new set of rules that will give *you* the advantage—rules that will not only make the game easier to play but will make the game financially and emotionally rewarding. You see, unlike what we have always been told, when it comes to buying a vehicle, it's *not* how you play the game, but whether you win or lose!

Some of what you are about to read will seem like nothing more than common sense, and quite frankly, that's because some of it is. Some of you will say to yourselves, "I wouldn't make those mistakes." Many of you think this way because you don't give enough consideration to what the term "salesperson" means. They're not called "purchase helpers," and for good reason. To many, a salesperson is little more than a good talker or someone who makes friends easily. In fact, this is the basis of a salesperson's ability to sell you. Some believe that their job depends on a good "personality," not training. A professional salesperson should be likened more to a surgeon. Someone who has been trained to "dissect" you, hold your life in their hands (in terms of profit and loss) and then has the ability to gain your trust and confidence. Believe me, like any doctor, a salesperson knows exactly where your jugular vein is, but unlike a doctor, many salespeople will cut it at their first opportunity.

The first step in changing the rules is to show you how to *buy* an automobile, not be *sold* one. To accomplish this, this guide will expose *how, what, where* and *when* car dealerships and salespeople actually go after and make their profits. It will then supply you with the tools and information you'll need to turn the table and play the game by your rules. Throughout, I have provided "AutoSave Tips," highlighting the most important ways you can save time, money and effort.

If you follow this guide—and I repeat that you should read the entire book—you will not only discover that your next automotive purchase or lease will be the "best deal" that you ever made, but that you made the experience easier and a lot more pleasurable.

Some things never change!

From 1992 through 1995 I wrote the first edition of this book. It was published and released in June of 1995. Since that time I have been interviewed on more than 100 television shows and more than 200 radio shows, plus numerous print interviews. Over and over again my interviewers keep asking me the same question: "But Kurt, isn't the automotive sales industry getting better? Aren't they now concentrating more on customer satisfaction in an attempt to clean up their image and gain more consumer respect and confidence?" The answer is not quite a simple yes or no. In almost all cases, we as consumers base our decisions 80 percent on "perception" and only 20 percent on actual facts. I may get you to "perceive" that something is better, but the fact may be that nothing has actually changed. A good example was the "new and improved" product advertising that was used extensively years ago. As consumers, we perceived that we were being offered a new and improved product and made our purchase decisions based on what the advertising lead us to perceive. The "facts" were, as it was later revealed, that the only thing that was "new and improved" was the packaging—the box the product came in—not the product itself. This is what I see today regarding the automotive sales industry. The "sharks" that are out there haven't suddenly become vegetarians. Your wallet, your money, is still their main diet, only the window dressing has changed. In fairness to the automotive sales industry, the answer to the original question would have to be yes. They are trying to improve customer satisfaction and clean up their image. But does this mean that they are not going to do everything they can to separate you from as much of your money as they can? The answer is a definitive no!

The biggest problem the consumer faces is not what to buy, but from whom and how to buy it. An automobile is still one of the few products for which we have to negotiate. Increased competition has caused dealerships to take large profit losses on the sale of their vehicles. So where, then, have they turned to make their profits? Parts and service departments are two areas that have seen tremendous price and labor increases, but a dealership is still not going to run its sales department at a loss.

Due to the easy availability of dealer "cost" and dealer "referral" services, car dealerships have been forced to concentrate more heavily on a profit area known as the "back-end." This area will often account for two-thirds or more of the profit they will make on you. This profit stems from how you choose to pay for your vehicle and what you purchase along with it. Most consumers shop little more than the price of the vehicle itself, but you will discover how and why the back-end represents such a large profit area for dealerships. You see, it is becoming more and more difficult for dealerships to mislead on the basis of selling price, but the back-end is still full of money-making opportunities.

The deceptions that are being aimed at the consumer today are not just from the dealerships or salespeople. The advertising used by the automobile manufacturers can also be very misleading. Sure, they will defend themselves by stating that what they are doing is within the confines of the law. But that doesn't help consumers much when few of them understand the conditions and disclaimers used in advertisements, and even if they did, few can see or hear these conditions and disclaimers in the way they're presented. Disclaimers in television advertisements that appear so fast that Evelyn Wood (the speed-reading instructor) couldn't read on her best day! Sentences spoken so fast on radio commercials that it sounds as if one giant word is being spoken or that we have been invaded by fast-talking aliens! Or how about print so small in newspapers that even those of us with 20/20 vision need a magnifying glass to read.

No, some things will never change, and the quest for the almighty dollar is certainly one of them. I know because I've been there. I live in that world. This book is simply my opportunity to give back a little of what I have participated in taking. If you ever really wanted an "insider's" guide to the automotive sales industry, look no further— you have it in your hands right now!

Chapter 1

The "best deal"

What is the "best deal"?

Throughout this guide, you will hear all or part of the following phrase numerous times, and for good reason. It is the most important consideration in getting the "best deal."

"The reliability and reputation of whom you do business with are the key factors to your purchase experience and ownership satisfaction. While you are certainly entitled to get a competitive price, remember that price isn't everything and that you usually get what you pay for."

This is what I would consider "profound" knowledge. Something that we all pretty much know, but don't always practice. If this was not the case, then we would all be shopping at "flea markets," and Nordstrom, Macy's and every other nice store that we shop at would have been out of business a long time ago. Eating out at restaurants is another instance in which we are willing to pay for atmosphere and quality service. And yet, even though many consumer surveys show that "you," the consumer, place price as low as 4th when making an automotive purchase decision, why is it that by the time you enter the dealership, like tunnel-vision, "price" is the only thing that you claim you are concerned with? The point here is that if you just stop beating yourself up over the automotive shopping experience and simply apply some of the considerations that motivate you when making other purchase decisions, you will greatly enhance your overall ownership experience. Isn't this what it is really all about? The shopping part only boils down to a couple of hours or days, while the ownership part can last for years to come. That couple of hundred dollars, or a few dollars a month, that you saved yourself by shopping price to death, was it all really worth it? Did you enjoy your shopping experience? Is the dealership you purchased from really going to be there when you need them for service? The answer to all of the above is, "very rarely."

I define the "best deal" as a combination of service, convenience and price, in that order.

It is not until you discover that the "best deal" is really more than just price that you can hope to become a truly satisfied consumer.

By taking the time and effort to research your options before you make decisions, you will end up with the right product, purchased from the right dealership, for the right price. The best way to do this is to be prepared. You must have the proper tools to make a good purchase decision. Not until you know exactly what you want and how and where you want to get it, can you truly go out and *buy* something instead of being *sold* it.

How do you get the "best deal"?

By taking the time to read this book, you are already on your way. The first thing you need to understand is that the automobile industry is constantly changing. No automobile will always be, or has always been, the best. The same holds true for the car dealership. Something or someone that was good in the past may not be today, or vice versa. This idea must also be applied to how you shop. The experiences you, your friends or your family might have had in the past cannot be the only reason you choose a vehicle or a dealership today. These past experiences should only be a small part of your decision-making process.

Today's technology can make rapid changes in the looks and quality of a vehicle. Manufacturers often completely change a product, yet never change the product's name. The same principle applies to car dealerships. Their names may stay the same, but their owners or management may not. One person's idea of good business may be completely different from another. (For more on this topic, see the sections "What is the 'right' vehicle?" on page 27 and "Choosing the 'right' dealership" in Chapter 2 on page 46.)

What about price?

Consumers always seem to be looking for a way to get one dealership to save them hundreds, even thousands of dollars compared to the quoted or selling price of another dealership. This is a natural buying habit with products for which we have to negotiate. When a deal is concluded, most consumers believe they could have gotten a better price had they been more persistent in their negotiations. The fact is, the difference between dealerships' actual bottom-line selling prices is rarely more than a couple of hundred dollars. Consumers, however, are led to believe otherwise by the misleading techniques some dealerships use, such as "low-balling." A "low-ball" is when you are given a "low price" for which a dealership has no intention of delivering you a vehicle. (Low-balls, which are used in many parts of the sales process, are discussed further in Chapter 3, page 83.)

Although many salespeople would like you to think otherwise, all dealerships do pay the same price for their automobiles! Except for an occasional manufacturer-to-dealer incentive program, any dealerships that have identically equipped vehicles have paid the exact same price for them. This holds true regardless of the size or volume of the dealership itself. In fact if you think about it, how else could national publications offer you what "dealer invoice" is if every dealership did not pay the same amount?

Small variations can occur from state to state, depending on transportation fees or dealers' contributions to lemon laws. Different "sales regions" throughout the country may also have different incentive programs and/or package discounts.

AutoSave Tip

You may be aware of a dealer profit area known as "hold-back." This is a flat percentage, normally about 3 percent of a vehicle's invoice, that is given back to the dealer and adds to his overall profits. Because dealer hold-back is rarely, if ever, used in negotiations with retail consumers, it should not be considered part of getting the "best deal." However, when the next model year of a vehicle is introduced, most automobile dealerships receive an additional kickback, about 5 percent of dealer invoice, from the manufacturer to help them move their leftovers, making actual dealer cost approximately 8 percent less than dealer invoice. Both the hold-back and the 5 percent leftover money should become part of your negotiations if the vehicle is a "leftover." You should try to negotiate at least 3 to 5 percent as added savings to you. (It should be noted that not all dealer brands practice "hold-back" price structuring. The practice is primarily with domestic automobiles.)

It is still difficult for some consumers to believe that dealerships pay the same price because it goes against the grain of how most businesses operate: The more they sell, the less they have to pay for the product. Realize that if this were true in the automobile sales industry, every small or average-sized car dealership would have been out of business years ago!

Some consumers respond to this with the notion that, although all dealerships pay the same price, if they sell more, they can afford to make less on each sale. The fact of the matter is that very few dealerships could stay in business if they relied only on the profit they make from the sale of the vehicle itself. Service, Parts, Finance and After-Sell departments are all important in how automobile dealerships earn their profits.

There are numerous reasons why you will find even slight differences in the selling price of a vehicle from one dealership to another. Some simply have more confidence in their ability to make back-end profits. Sometimes, what seems to be a difference in a quoted price is actually a low-ball. Other dealerships simply invest more money into customer service and satisfaction, and they require the extra profits to do so.

Without the purchase of a "price guide," a basic guideline can be used to approximate dealer invoice. If you use a price guide, don't count on it being totally accurate. Many leave out areas of dealer costs, such as mandatory advertising funds or transportation fees. Another problem is that manufacturers often have more than one price increase during a model year, and your publication may not be up-to-date. Dealer cost publications and services, in most cases, should be used only as a basic guideline. My experience has shown that in most cases, prices offered by these publications are rarely accurate.

The profit margin guideline on page 22 also should not be considered completely accurate. The following percentages are based strictly on an average markup derived from my own personal sales experience with both import and domestic vehicles. Manufacturers' actual markups on vehicles vary. The dollar figures shown here represent the markup between dealer invoice and Manufacturer's Suggested Retail Price (M.S.R.P.). They do not take into account any dealer or consumer incentive programs. M.S.R.P. is also defined as the price listed at the bottom of the window sticker, *after* the package discounts that most automobiles have from the manufacturer. (Package discounts are discussed in Chapter 3.)

Profit Margin Guideline

M.S.R.P. of Vehicle	Profit Margin
$12,000 and under	7%- 9%
$12,000 to $20,000	9%-11%
$20,000 to $30,000	11%-15%
$30,000 and over	15%-20%

Because it takes little effort to get a good price on a vehicle, and because price ranks last in my definition of the "best deal," let's take a look at how paying a small amount more at one dealership than you would at another just might offer you more for your money.

Mechanics. It costs more to hire the best, but those dealerships that do can save you a lot of time, money and aggravation in the long run. Many dealerships will also invest in ongoing training to ensure that their mechanics are kept up-to-date with the latest technologies of today's automobiles.

Service equipment. A service department's inability to quickly find or fix a problem is usually due to a lack of proper tools. Tools, like automobiles, have become more technical and costly. The inability to properly diagnose or fix a problem is the *number-one* service complaint that consumers have.

Parts. Stocking parts that are rarely needed is a financial burden, but the dealership that stocks these parts will be able to offer faster and better service.

Prepped vehicles. Some dealerships, although they are paid to prep (perform a pre-delivery inspection of) their vehicles by automobile manufacturers, will haphazardly prep their vehicles before delivering them to their customers, if they prep them at all. Neglecting to properly prep a vehicle is one of the leading causes of initial vehicle breakdowns.

Professionalism. Better dealerships will invest a lot of money into the training of their employees. Some go as far as investing in a full-time "Customer Relations Representative." This type of investment can offer you, the customer, a much greater level of overall satisfaction.

Service hours. Highly trained mechanics are very well-paid. It is costly to a dealership to offer extended service hours, such as evenings or weekends, but of course, these extended service hours can offer you, the customer, a much greater level of convenience.

All of the items that I listed above can and will improve your long-term and overall level of ownership satisfaction. Once again, most of us are willing to pay a little extra for quality service, why not with the car dealership?

I have often been questioned about my statement that the difference in the actual selling price of the vehicle itself between dealerships is rarely more than a couple of hundred dollars. I have heard hundreds of stories from consumers who are convinced that one dealership saved them thousands of dollars as compared to another. It is important to understand what the word "deception" means. If a salesperson has successfully deceived you, you may never be aware of what, where, when or how he or she did it. I would guess that 90 percent of the consumers who have been deceived will never know it and will continue to believe that they got a good deal. It is the use of deception that probably represents most of the confusion consumers seem to have regarding dealer markup and actual selling price.

AutoSave Tip

Many dealerships throughout the country are still trying to sell the "haggle- (or hassle-) free" approach to car sales. With this concept, a dealership will mark its vehicles with one selling price that is not supposed to be negotiable. The main problem with this type of selling is that it attempts to focus the consumer's thoughts and shopping habits on the idea that "price" is the most important concern. By doing this, it attempts to keep the consumer's concentration away from the "big picture"—the dealerships's efforts to make back-end profits. Remember that few things are carved in stone. Almost every "haggle-free" dealership that I have known still leaves room in prices for negotiating. The concept of haggle-free is once again an attempt by the automobile sales industry to make sure that you play the game by its rules, not yours, so it can keep the advantage.

Summary

Basically, what I have talked about up to this point is understanding that the "best deal" and the "best price" are not always the same thing. There is a lot more involved with the purchase of an automobile than simply going from dealership to dealership asking, "What's your best price?" I can't stress enough the importance of understanding that the reliability and reputation of whom you do business with are truly going to be the keys to your overall satisfaction. And I repeat that my definition of the "best deal" is service, convenience and price, in that order.

Hopefully, you have realized by now that dealerships do pay the same price for their vehicles regardless of their size or volume of business, and perhaps more importantly, you have realized that most vehicles do not have the tremendous amount of markup that many consumers believe they do. So, what are your new rules for playing the game so far?

1. Never shop price! Shop the quality and convenience of the dealership.

2. Never shop price! Find out what the dealer invoice is on the vehicle(s) you are considering, and then when you have chosen the right dealership, simply tell the salesperson what you are willing to pay for the vehicle.

3. Never shop price! Period!

Once again, realize that it is not how much over invoice a dealership sells a vehicle that determines its profitability on the sale. It is the other area referred to earlier, and explained in more detail later on, known as the back-end that helps to make up the entire dealer profit structure. It is not until you can closely examine the entire deal that you received on a vehicle that you can determine whether you really got the "best deal."

Chapter 2

First things first

Before you start to shop

Automotive salespeople are trained to win. You may be great in the supermarket, appliance or clothing store, but it is a mistake to believe anything other than the fact that car salespeople have the advantage. They get to practice and improve their skills every day. Only by taking an organized approach to making your automotive purchases will you truly become a more satisfied customer and be able to make the "best deal."

The first point to understand is that the sales process does not end when you give your deposit. In fact, to the dealership, it has only just begun. Some of the following techniques will seem familiar. This is because they are ways that you already shop for other things. You simply haven't applied them enough, or properly, to purchasing an automobile.

Shopping list, budget, research and being prepared

Few people go to the supermarket without a shopping list. You spend the time deciding what products you want to buy before you go shopping. Many of the items on your list, or the brands that you choose, reflect a budget that you have. Many consumers even do research. They may be concerned with their diets and only look to buy food that is good for them. Some simply read the cans or boxes to compare brands or check out the ingredients. These same shopping skills need to be applied to purchasing a vehicle. You need to know exactly what you are going to buy and what your budget is and then do some research before you start your shopping so you can make the right decisions.

Most consumers walk into a car dealership unprepared because they don't know what they want. They are not prepared for all that the dealership has in store for them. These shoppers accept what they are *led* to believe is a good deal. They think that by visiting a few dealerships they can sort out the information and make a good buying decision. They expect that the car salesperson is going to inform and help them. If car salespeople were actually there to help, they might have been called "purchase helpers" instead of "car salespeople."

Being prepared is the tough part. Only by knowing how and what the salesperson is going to try to do can you be ready. There are good shoppers out there who take the time to check a vehicle out. They look into its reputation, read the magazines and maybe even research its cost. The problem is that they stop there. They don't take the entire "big picture" into consideration. But dealerships do, and this is why they continue to win. Unlike picking out a brand of cereal, a vehicle is much more than the product itself. Your shopping list needs to include items such as: what options you desire or need, servicing considerations and, most importantly, how you are going to pay for the vehicle. When your shopping list includes all of the areas of your purchase, you will be able to use the "big picture" and will have the necessary information to go out and *buy* a vehicle instead of being *sold* one, and of course, you'll be able to get the "best deal." There is an example of a shopping list form on page 182 that you should find helpful.

Summary

What are the new rules you should have learned?

1. Be prepared! Don't be led by car salespeople. They are there to sell. You are there to buy—and that is not the same thing!
2. Be prepared! Remember to always keep the "big picture" in mind. Have your shopping list, budget and research done before you ever visit a car dealership.
3. Be prepared! Don't expect a salesperson to help you. You have got to help yourself. If you are fortunate enough to choose a salesperson who really is helpful, that should simply be considered a bonus to your own efforts, not a replacement for them.

What is the "right" vehicle?

It may sound simplistic to say that the right vehicle is one that fulfills your needs and wants at a budget that you are comfortable with. Unfortunately, many consumers complain that they are not satisfied with their vehicles. This is because they were *sold* something instead of making a *buying* decision. They leave too much to impulse decisions that are helped along by the car dealerships' sales and management teams.

Listed below are some of the basics you should decide on before you ever visit a car dealership.

1. Do I want or need two doors, four doors, a station wagon, a minivan or even a truck?

2. How many passengers will usually be in my vehicle?

3. Where do I do most of my driving? Mountains, city, country, etc. (Power-train consideration.)

4. How many miles per year will I most likely drive? (Fuel economy consideration.)

5. What are the basic options I require? (Automatic or manual transmission, air conditioning and so forth.)

6. Will I be towing or carrying anything, and if so, how much, how often and for what distance?

7. How much will this purchase affect my insurance premiums? (An extremely important issue few consumers check out before they go car shopping.)

8. What exactly is my monthly budget? (Discussed in the section "Establishing a budget" on page 38.)

9. What other extras do I want or need? (Extended warranties, alarms, etc.)

These are all very important questions that need to be answered before you ever start to shop for a vehicle. This guide will help you to decide on these considerations and then help you to make out a shopping list that you should use to stick to the decisions that you have made. In other words, you will have something to refer to when you are being influenced by the expertise of a salesperson.

Import or domestic?

Want to start an argument? Just find one person who believes in "Buy American" and another who only buys imports. Opinions will fly, but unfortunately, most of them will have little to do with reality. The issue of import or domestic has become a confusing one. Just what is an import or a domestic vehicle?

Did you know that for a vehicle to claim "Made in America," it has to contain only 51 percent of American-built parts? Automobile manu-facturers have turned the question of import or domestic into more of a sales pitch than anything else. Many domestic brand-name vehicles are not built in the United States, while many import brand-name vehicles are. To complicate matters further, many imports are re-named and sold in domestic automobile showrooms, while the trend of renaming domestic vehicles and selling them in import showrooms also grows. The domestic manufacturers, once known as the "big three," all have strong ties with Japanese and other foreign manufac-turers. Many of today's vehicles, and future ones, are products of joint ventures between these companies. Because a brand name does not necessarily denote whether the vehicle is an import or domestic, how do we choose? Let's take a look at a few of the areas that actually mo-tivate our purchase decisions.

Quality. I would be one of the first to agree that a decade or so ago, the Japanese and Europeans built a better vehicle and offered it at a better value (cost). But that was then, and this is now! When Japanese manufacturers started to penetrate the American market with cheap and reliable vehicles in the 1970s, it put a sizable dent into domestic auto sales. U.S. production methods were outdated and the Japanese were offering new and innovative products. By the mid-1980s, the U.S. car makers had little choice: update or continue to lose market share. Update they did, and today's U.S. automobile plants can rival those of any manufacturer in the world. As one of the "big three" likes to put it, quality became "Job 1," and thanks to the ex-tensive use of computers and robots, the day of the "Monday morning hangover car" is a thing of the past. Basically, there are little to no dif-ferences in quality between domestic and import vehicles anymore. Sure, there are certain imports that offer the "best" that can be had. There are no $100,000 domestic vehicles to compete with a top-of-the-line Mercedes...yet. As consumer confidence in domestic manufactur-ers grows, I am sure that we will see this level of competition in the not-so-distant future.

Although most of us have been told that we must learn from the past, when it comes to a fast-paced, fast-changing industry like automobile manufacturing, we have to remember not to lose sight of the present. If you are shopping for quality, research the *current* reputation of a vehicle. *Don't* rely on its past merits.

Value. Up until the mid-1980s the strong U.S. dollar gave imports a considerable price advantage. Even with price "gouging," which led many consumers to pay more than the actual M.S.R.P. of a vehicle, many consumers still found value with imports. But once again, that was then, and this is now! The U.S. dollar no longer has the strength it once did. Japanese vehicles no longer have ridiculously low sticker prices, and in fact, there is certainly no price advantage to any import in today's economy.

Unfortunately, no matter how much the prices of imports go up, no matter how much better Americans produce their vehicles, many consumers, being the creatures of habit that they are, still blindly go out shopping with imports as their only consideration. The attitude of habit is that if it were good for me yesterday, then it should be good for me today. This is a definite mistake when you are attempting to make an educated decision. I'm not suggesting that you *have* to buy Amer-ican, just that you should simply keep up with the changes and at least look before saying no.

Loyalty. Because without extensive product research it is difficult to tell whether you are buying an imported or a domestic vehicle, the question of loyalty can be problematic. You may want to be loyal to America and buy American. But what is an American vehicle? Is it a vehicle with an American manufacturer's nameplate that is actually built in Canada, Mexico, Korea or even Japan, or is it a vehicle with a foreign manufacturer's nameplate that is built in the United States? Loyalty alone is not a good basis for getting good value for your money. With the average automobile today listing for more than $20,000, your buying decisions need to be based on researching the value and quality of all the brands that are within your budget. The same concept of loyalty holds true when considering any brand. Perhaps you or your family always bought Fords, Hondas, Chevys or whatever the brand might be, but this type of product loyalty has no place in making a good buying decision. Once again, you should be looking at all of the brands that offer vehicles that fall within your budget.

To sum it all up, these days a "nameplate" may have little to do with what you are actually buying. If quality and value are your main criteria, you must forget about the concept of import or domestic and base your decision solely on the individual merits of the vehicle and the dealership that you are purchasing it from.

Comparing brands

As just discussed, advances in technology have helped to make our decisions easier. No longer do we have to be as concerned with who is building a better product. Many of our decisions can now be more emotional and financial. More than ever, the key to getting the "best deal" is not what you buy, but how and from what dealership you buy it.

You are about to spend thousands of dollars to own a product that you will spend hundreds of hours in, put your life at stake with, depend on for many reasons and, hopefully, enjoy—usually for years. Spending time doing research is a must! Automobiles are too expensive a proposition to be left to an emotional buying decision instead of an educated one.

AutoSave Tip

There are many vehicles to choose from in everyone's price range. The more you investigate your choices and educate yourself about them, the more satisfied you will be with your final decision.

Once you have established your budget (refer to "Establishing a budget" on page 38) and you know exactly what price range you should be looking at, make a list of the cars that fall within this range. There are dozens of magazines and publications that can help you with this. Just go to any bookstore, newsstand or library and you will find them. Once your list is made, it is time to take a closer look at your choices. At this point you should not be deciding on a brand or a dealership. You should simply spend a couple of hours visiting show-rooms to view your choices. You should sit in them, *test drive* them and take a brochure. No decisions should be made at this point. The only help that you should accept from the salesperson is to have him or her show you the vehicle and to fill you in on any current incentive programs. A "brand comparison form" on page 179 can help you keep track of your notes.

After you have finished checking out your choices, they should be narrowed down to only two or three vehicles. The next step is to find out who builds them and the other nameplates under which they might be sold. Almost every manufacturer markets its vehicles under more than one name. The variations in the product itself are usually very minor and are often more cosmetic than mechanical. The brand name the vehicle is sold under can affect its price or the type of deal you can make. Because many consumers are familiar with "import restrictions," the foreign car showroom will often try to hold out for bigger profits. Here are just two examples out of dozens of vehicles that are cross-marketed.

1. A Toyota Corolla and a Geo Prism, for all practical pur-poses, are the same car; both are built by Toyota. Because foreign car buyers perceive greater value with imports, they are more likely to pay more for the import nameplate. Prism is sold in Chevrolet/Geo franchises.

2. The Mercury Sable and the Ford Taurus are virtually the same car; both are built by Ford. Here, Ford sells the idea that Mercury is a more upscale product.

An issue that is often raised is resale value. One might say that the import nameplate will have better resale value than the domestic one. In many cases, this is true. You need to consider how much more you might have to spend up front in order to *hopefully* get more back later.

The cycle of R & D and quality

In most cases, any given model automobile will go through changes about every three to five years. From the manufacturers' standpoint, this period will usually contain a cycle of research and development and quality control. The idea that the first model year of a product is not the best is often not far from the truth. Regardless of the efforts a manufacturer may take to make its product great from the start, most of the product's inception costs have been spent on research and development. It's not until a vehicle has been in the hands of the consumer for a while that the unexpected arises. The next couple of years are when most of the effort on quality control is placed. If a product has done at least fairly well, the profits from its last couple of years, before it is redesigned, will usually go back into the R & D of its upcoming version.

AutoSave Tip
Based on my experience, the best time to purchase any given model is between the second and fourth year that version has been in production.

Options you should be considering

Although many options on a vehicle are considered more wants than needs, certain options can affect your vehicle's resale value and *ease* of sale.

Automatic transmission (cars). With today's fuel efficient engines, automatic transmissions now offer almost the same fuel economy as a manual transmission. Other than in sports cars, a manual transmission can greatly reduce a vehicle's resale value. Most automatic transmissions will add between $700 and $1,200 to your purchase price. Without this option, your loss in wholesale, retail or trade-in value will usually range between $1,000 and $2,000. In other words, an automatic transmission will usually pay for itself.

Automatic transmission (trucks). If you intend to have more than one person drive your truck, even if they are experienced drivers, you should be considering an automatic transmission. The wear and tear of different driving styles on the clutch of a manual transmission can cause a lot of replacement costs and downtime.

Many consumers are under the impression that if they intend to be towing something, they need a manual transmission. This is definitely not true! Most automatic transmissions can tow twice as much as manual transmissions. In fact, most automobile (and truck) manufacturers advise against towing with manual transmissions altogether. All manufacturers offer towing guidelines for their vehicles. If you do intend to tow, examine these guidelines closely and be sure to enlist the aid of a qualified salesperson.

AutoSave Tip

My experience has shown me that vehicles with a manual transmission not only drop in resale value but are some of the most difficult to resell used. Because clutches in *new* vehicles are not even covered by a warranty, consumers are afraid of a greater potential for problems and costly repairs when looking at a used vehicle with a manual transmission.

Air conditioning. A vehicle without air conditioning will lose an average of $1,000 to $2,500 in resale or trade-in value. New, the option usually costs only $800 to $1,000.

Power convenience. The absence of options such as power windows and door locks can present a problem with the resale of vehicles that are generally considered luxury cars. Consumers who shop for used luxury cars consider these options a must. Your loss in resale value can be as much as or more than the original cost to purchase these options.

Safety equipment. Although options such as air bags, side impact intrusion beams and anti-lock brakes do not necessarily reflect themselves in resale or trade-in value, much of their original cost to you may be deferred through insurance discounts. What cost do you place on the safety of you and your passengers?

Antitheft systems. Options such as alarms may offer a small return in resale value but, as with safety equipment, they too may have much of their original cost deferred through insurance discounts.

Cargo and towing capacity (trucks). Increased payload options on trucks can cost as little as $50. These options may provide more than you need but can offer you a much greater advantage when you look to sell your vehicle. Most towing packages range between $150 and $350 and can affect the resale value of your vehicle about the same amount. In other words, the small price that you will pay up front for these options can greatly increase the market for potential buyers when you are looking to sell your vehicle.

Extended warranties. Most extended warranties are transferable to the second owner of a vehicle for a nominal fee. This can greatly increase your ease of resale, along with how much you can ask for your vehicle.

AutoSave Tip

If you trade in a vehicle before the extended warranty expires or sell the vehicle without transferring it to the new owner, you can usually cancel it and receive a prorated refund of its original purchase price. You should look into this at the time you are considering buying the warranty.

Considering used?

With many automobiles now costing more than most homes did just a couple of generations ago, more consumers are considering a used vehicle than ever before. The first thought that often comes to mind is, "Do I want someone else's headache?" The issue to remember here is that even new vehicles can have problems. A good used vehicle can be just as reliable as a new one. As far as cost of ownership is concerned, you should read the section "The economics of a used vehicle purchase" on page 151 in Chapter 7. Let's take a look at why a used vehicle may be a consideration.

Reliability. If you are considering used as an alternative to new, then you want a vehicle that is only one to three years old. The quality of most new vehicles has greatly increased in just the last five years. Even if a vehicle had a problem when it was traded in, reputable dealerships will have it corrected before it is put up for sale. This can mean that a vehicle that might have been a problem to the first owner when it was new could end up not being a problem to you as a used vehicle.

Warranties. Most manufacturers' warranties remain on a vehicle for the duration of their term or mileage, even after the original owner has sold or traded in the vehicle. If you are looking at a late-model used vehicle, odds are that it will still have the balance of the original factory warranty. Because of this, dealerships are required to perform an extensive check-out on the vehicle before they can offer it for sale.

Used vehicle extended warranties are also available. Because the sale of used vehicle warranties is another source of dealership income, dealerships often don't volunteer to tell you if the used vehicle you are considering has a balance left on the factory warranty. Ask!

AutoSave Tip

If you notice a vehicle on a used car lot marked with a sticker stating that it has the balance of the original new vehicle warranty, be sure to ask specifically what the warranty covers. As an example, the emissions control system on most vehicles is covered longer than the rest of the vehicle. Because this is an item covered by the automobile manufacturer, some dealerships will state that a vehicle has the balance of its original factory warranty—a statement that may lead you to believe that more is being covered than actually is.

Economics. Most vehicles will depreciate 10 percent to 30 percent in just the first year. By considering a late model used vehicle, someone else will have taken this loss instead of you. Refer to the section "The economics of a used vehicle purchase" on page 151 in Chapter 7.

Needs and wants. Because a used vehicle will sell for a lot less than its same version new, it offers you the opportunity to purchase a more fully equipped vehicle. Refer to Chapter 7 for more detailed information on buying a used car.

Summary

There were many important issues discussed in this section. One of the most important was to realize that we are creatures of habit—that we base many of our buying decisions on our past experiences. In addition, statistically we base 80 percent of our decisions on *perception* and only 20 percent on fact. In other words, what you think you see is not always what you end up getting. This is something you have to try to avoid when it comes to shopping for an automobile. The industry is changing all the time. Buying out of habit is like being blindfolded and playing "pin the tail on the donkey." Unfortunately, the automobile industry has the pin, and you will end up being the donkey. If you are still not sure what the right vehicle is going to be for you, then I suggest that you read the next section on establishing your budget and then reread this section.

I will also repeat that it is very important that you read this entire book from beginning to end. Although each chapter can be used as reference material, the book is designed to help you create a much bigger picture of the shopping and buying experience than you've probably had before. What new rules, then, should you have learned from this section?

1. Determine your wants and needs in a vehicle before you go shopping. Remember that you want to *buy* what you want, not be *sold* what they want.

2. Forget about the question of import or domestic. It is irrelevant in today's marketplace. Research all the brands within your budget.

3. Find out what other nameplates or brand names the vehicle(s) you are considering are sold under. This can often save you a great deal of money.

4. When determining your wants and needs in a vehicle, remember that certain options cost less to buy up front than the amount you might lose when you are ready to trade in or sell your vehicle.

5. Buying a used vehicle does not necessarily mean purchasing someone else's headache. Used vehicles can be an alternative to new. More is explained in Chapter 7.

Establishing a budget

Budgets can be easy to develop but are often difficult to keep. In fact, I would venture to guess that at least 95 percent of consumers to whom I have sold vehicles ended up spending more than the budget they had in mind when I first met them. Much of this is simply because few budgets are established with the "big picture" in mind, remembering items such as sales tax, motor vehicle fees, warranties and numerous other items that are often not originally considered but easily become part of exceeding your budget. Salespeople, of course, are trained to deal with this. They always attempt to use the smallest possible figure: "I know, Mr. and Mrs. Smith, that you planned to spend only $300 a month, and this vehicle is $325. But realize that the difference represents less than a dollar a day. You probably spend more than that on coffee, don't you?" Oh, yes! That "less than a dollar a day" sure sounds better than an extra $25 a month, doesn't it? And believe me, that kind of sales technique works very well. The key here, of course, is knowing up front what you intend to buy and what its *total* cost will be.

Along with the guidelines shown at the end of this section, the back of this guide has loan amortization tables with instructions that can help you outline and determine your monthly payments on a conventional loan.

The following are some of the basic expenses that consumers often overlook when considering a budget.

Insurance. Almost always, a new vehicle will mean higher insurance premiums. The model of the vehicle alone can greatly affect your cost to insure it. Most finance companies require that you have full coverage on your vehicle, which includes collision, not just liability coverage. You should call your insurance agent and find out exactly how much the vehicle(s) you are considering will change your current premiums. You should also ask him or her about available discounts for vehicles that are equipped with air bags, passive restraint systems, anti-theft devices or any other options or products that may offer you a discount on your premiums.

Maintenance. New or used, vehicles cost money to maintain. Be ready for unexpected repairs. Ask your dealer about routine maintenance costs. Services such as tune-ups and oil changes should all be a part of your budget. Maintenance is one of the first items passed over when the original budget didn't include it. Skipping an occasional oil change, tune-up or routine maintenance inspection, or waiting until your tires are almost bald before you replace them, may leave a few extra dollars in your pocket today, but odds are it will cost you even more in the long run.

Numerous surveys have shown that as of the third year of vehicle ownership, or beyond its 30,000 mile point, most consumers can expect to spend $100 to $125 per month, on the average, in routine maintenance expenses. These include basics such as new tires, shocks, muffler and tune-ups. In other words, if you purchase a new vehicle with a loan more than two years long that costs you $250 per month, your cost of ownership from the third year on will more realistically be about $350 per month. This is one of the reasons why consumers are increasingly turning to short-term leases, which will be discussed further on.

Down payment. Always leave enough aside for the unexpected. Never make a down payment with more money than you are comfortable being without. Creative ways of financing, such as leasing or balloon notes, can help solve some common down-payment problems.

Accessories. Options such as extended warranties and alarms can greatly add to your budget, although some of them may help with maintaining or lowering your overall expenses of ownership.

Use the following worksheet to create and establish your budget.

How much can you afford?

Follow the instructions on the next page before you start to fill in any numbers.

(A) Maximum Monthly Budget ....= $_____
(B) Insurance $_____ + Maintenance $__ ____ ....= $_____
    (A) minus (B) = Maximum Loan Payment.................= $_____
(C) Maximum Down Payment..= $_____
(D) Amount you can finance for _____ months..............= $_____
    (C) plus (D) = Maximum price range of car ....= $_____

Have I Got a Deal for You!

Instructions

(A) Should equal your total budget for a car based on your income and normal expenses. A rule of thumb is to never allow this amount to be greater than one week's "net" income.

(B) Insurance should be based on actual quotes and broken down into a monthly amount. Maintenance will have to be approximated. The following are examples of normal maintenance expenses. Prices should be checked locally.

The following examples are based on driving 60,000 miles a year during a 48-month loan:

Oil change every 3,000 miles	20 @ $25 each	= $500
Tune-ups at 30,000 miles	2 @ $200 each	= $400
Brakes at 20,000 miles	3 @ $150 each	= $450
Tires at 40,000 miles	4 @ $125 each	= $500
Miscellaneous (such as exhaust, belts, hoses, etc.)		= $500
		Total = $2,350

$2,350 divided by 48 months = $48.96 to be added to your monthly budget based on the above example. (Remember to add this figure to whatever insurance figure you came up with before you fill in the line B total).

(A) minus (B) should be the maximum loan payment that you consider.

(C) You must decide what down payment you are comfortable with.

(D) To determine how much you can finance, first decide the "term" (length of the loan) that you are comfortable with. As an example, we will say that you decided on a maximum loan payment of $275 per month, you want a 36-month loan and the average interest rate is 9 percent. If you turn to the loan amortization tables in the back of the guide (pages 176-177), and look up 9 percent for 36 months, you will find a payment factor of .031800. Start off by multiplying the factor times $10,000 and you will see that it gives you a payment of $318 per month, which is more than you wanted to spend. Reduce the amount that you multiply times the .031800 until you come as close as possible to the $275 payment that you wanted. It may take a couple of attempts to get the right figure, but for this example, you will come up with the figure of $8,650.

(C) plus (D) By adding the amount that you can finance to your maximum down payment, you will see the exact total amount that you have to spend. Don't forget about sales tax!

Summary

Once again, in this section, the key to success is to remember that you must always keep the "big picture" in mind by realizing that there are a lot more costs involved in shopping for an automobile than the price of the automobile itself. Always look at your purchase with its complete, total cost in mind.

What are the new rules that you have learned here?

1. Establish your complete budget before you start to shop! Make sure that the budget includes everything I discussed.

2. Remember that salespeople are trained to break down costs to the smallest possible number so they sound better. One dollar a day still is, and will always be, $30 a month.

3. Stand by your budget decisions. Do not be sold or told by someone else how much you can afford!

Your current vehicle

Should you trade it or sell it privately?

Before deciding what you should do with your current vehicle, you must have a good idea of its value, whether you are going to retail it, wholesale it or trade it in. The average difference between wholesale and retail will generally range between $1,500 and $3,000. There are many other considerations you must look at. Listed here are a few of the most basic considerations:

Sales tax. Most states charge sales tax only on the amount of difference between your trade and the new vehicle purchase price. This tax savings adds value to your trade-in. For example, you are looking to purchase a $15,000 vehicle and your trade-in is worth $5,000. If your state charges 6 percent sales tax, you will pay that tax only on the $10,000 difference. The added value to your trade-in, then, is the 6 percent tax you saved on the $5,000, which is $300. In this case, if you decide to retail your car on your own, you must get at least $5,300 for it to match its trade-in value. This, of course, does not include any other additional expenses that you may incur, such as the cost of advertising the vehicle.

Advertising. How much will it cost you to sell your vehicle?

Time and convenience. Consider the value that you place on your personal time, along with the problems that are associated with selling a vehicle privately.

Incentive programs. Manufacturers' incentive programs have time limits. Taking the time to sell your vehicle privately could cause you to miss out on these savings.

Privacy. Selling your vehicle on your own usually means that you have to advertise it and give out your home telephone number. In addition, it also means that you will be giving strangers directions to your home.

It is unfortunate that in today's society we have to be so cautious, but caution is what I definitely recommend. Give plenty of thought to what is involved and what is at stake by attempting to sell your vehicle on your own.

How to determine the value of your current vehicle

Regardless of what you intend to do with your current vehicle, you must first take a realistic look at it. You know how it runs or what damage it has or might have had. Listed below are some important considerations.

Mileage. 12,000 to 15,000 miles per model year are generally considered average. Deductions for every extra 1,000 miles that your vehicle has will usually range from $60 for economy cars to $125 for luxury cars. With a private sale, you may be able to discuss your driving habits or how well you maintained your vehicle, but car salespeople are not going to listen or care. They are the ones who are going to have to sell it if you trade it, not you.

Appearance. Even color is a consideration. A red sports car is certainly more popular than a brown one and is going to be easier to sell. The exterior and interior appearance is very important. A good wash job may work for a private sale, but expect a salesperson to look beyond dirt. Burn holes, scratches, dings, windshield damage, and so on, are all things that a salesperson is going to use as "tools" to offer you less money. Many of these things can be touched up or repaired with little time or expense to you. This can add hundreds of dollars to your vehicle's value.

Often, a vehicle's windshield is damaged by small rocks or pebbles that are kicked up from the road surface by other vehicles. Usually, this type of damage is referred to as "bull's eyes" and "star breaks." When the car salesperson discovers this kind of damage on your vehicle's windshield, he or she will usually tell you that the windshield must be replaced. The cost, which represents a trade-in value deduction to you, will usually range from $300 to $800. However, numerous companies that can repair this type of damage—usually for $50 or less—are available to you and the dealership. Realizing that few consumers are aware of this repair procedure, the salesperson can often justify his or her trade-in value deduction of hundreds of dollars for a repair bill that is only going to cost a fraction of that.

Other companies can also repair minor dents on your vehicle. If these companies are not listed in your yellow pages, contact the used car manager of a local dealership and simply ask who he recommends for such services.

Additionally, many new products on the market can help to restore the finish on your vehicle. Usually costing less than $20, these pro-ducts can increase your vehicle's value by hundreds of dollars.

Popularity. In most cases, the more popular a vehicle is, the lower its resale value. This statement is based on the rule of supply and demand. A popular vehicle means that many of them have been sold. The more used ones available, the more competitive their selling price will be.

Running condition. Salespeople will check your oil, listen to the engine and usually test drive your trade-in. Most people who appraise trade-ins are not mechanics. They often have to guess about a potential problem. To protect themselves, this guess will usually represent the worst possible scenario, meaning the largest possible appraisal deduction to you.

AutoSave Tip

If your vehicle isn't running well, have it checked out by an independent mechanic and get a written estimate of what is actually wrong with it and the cost to repair it. This will give you a good guideline to compare what the salesperson claims is wrong and how much he wants to deduct for these problems.

The "four market values" of your current vehicle

Part of understanding what your current vehicle is worth is understanding that it has different values depending on what you choose to do with it. Listed here are what are generally considered the "four market values" of your vehicle:

1. Retail. This is the value for which you can sell your vehicle on your own. Publications such as the N.A.D.A. (National Automobile Dealers Association) official used car guide can be read at most banks, libraries or car dealerships. The numbers they show are only guidelines. The condition and marketability of the vehicle will determine its actual value.

AutoSave Tip

The best way to determine how much you should sell your vehicle for, if you have decided to retail it, is by looking in your local newspapers or publications that advertise used vehicles. Base your asking price on what people are asking for similar vehicles in your area.

---

2. Insurance. An insurance company is not the place to get the value of your vehicle. The guidelines they use are for estimating repair or replacement value due to accidents or theft. This value has little to do with the amount for which you can sell or trade your vehicle.

3. Loan. The value that a bank determines is the extent of funds they are willing to loan against any given vehicle. Like insurance value, it has little to do with the amount for which you can retail your vehicle. It is, however, close to or often used as a wholesale value by the dealership. The loan value of a vehicle, plus 20 percent, is a good gauge for judging its retail value. This can also be used as a guide to help determine the validity of a price a dealership is asking for a used vehicle. Loan values are usually listed in used car guides such as the one published by N.A.D.A.

4. Wholesale. This is the actual amount that a dealership or wholesaler is willing to pay for your vehicle. It is the foundation of trade-in value. Check with your local dealerships about which books or publications they use in your area to determine a vehicle's wholesale value. You should then be able to find that same book in your local library or be able to purchase it in a book or automotive store.

AutoSave Tip

Inform the dealership that you wish to *see* the book it is using to appraise your trade. These books are not secret documents. Salespeople don't offer to show them to you because the less you know, the better of an advantage they have.

If you are not comfortable with the trade value your dealership is offering, there can be an alternative. Some dealerships have less of a market for vehicles that don't fit into their type of business. One example would be trading in a full-sized luxury car for a smaller economy car. The economy car salesperson will have few people looking for a used luxury car. Because of this, he or she will most likely be shy on what he or she is willing to offer you for it. Keeping the possible loss of sales tax savings in mind, try bringing your vehicle to the dealership whose brand it is, and offering it for outright sale to that dealership. These same brand dealerships will often go over book value for a vehicle that fits their primary market. In some cases, dealerships will even work with each other to help you save on the sales tax. In a state that does not offer any sales tax savings on a trade-in, this procedure can become even more valuable to you.

Summary

It is very important to understand the "true" value of your current vehicle. Automobile salespeople and dealerships have always tried to play numbers games when it comes to trade-ins. They will often tell you that they are giving you more for your vehicle than the amount for which they have actually appraised it. They can do this by offering less of a discount on the new vehicle's selling price. For example, if a salesperson gives you a discount of only $1,000 on a vehicle that he or she could feasibly discount by $1,500, he or she could then show that you are getting $500 more for your trade-in—$500 that should really be part of your discount on the new vehicle.

Use the tools I supplied to place a realistic number on your vehicle based on whether you are going to trade it in or attempt to sell it on your own. What new rules should you have learned in this section?

1. You will always get more selling a vehicle on your own, but be sure to examine how much this will cost you in terms of time, advertising expenses and loss of privacy.
2. When a dealership has made an offer on your trade, ask to see the book used to determine that value. If you have done your homework, it should be the same book that you already checked out.
3. Whether or not you like the trade-in value a salesperson has offered you, take the time to bring your vehicle to its same brand dealership and offer it for sale. The same brand dealership is almost always willing to offer more for your vehicle. If you are already purchasing the same brand as your current vehicle, all the better.
4. Don't be fooled by numbers games. You don't have to keep it a secret that you have a trade-in, which is what so many other books and seminars are attempting to tell you. Just understand the actual trade-in value of your vehicle, and keep the selling price and trade negotiations separate.

Choosing the "right" dealership

There are few things we depend on more than our vehicles. We may spend more time using products such as telephones, televisions and so on, but no product that we use costs us as much, needs to be maintained as often or is subject to more problems than our vehicles. Choosing the right dealership will make you a more satisfied owner regardless of the actual vehicle you choose to buy. The purchase of a vehicle is a multi-year experience, and until you deal with the "big picture," you are doing little more than gambling with your level of satisfaction.

When it comes to choosing a dealership, big does not mean the same as best and certainly has nothing to do with the dealership's reputation or your overall level of satisfaction. I repeat that the reliability and reputation of whom you do business with will be the keys to your satisfaction.

Some consumers have little choice as to whom they buy from. Except in metropolitan areas, the choice of a particular brand may leave you with only one dealership to choose from in your area. This guide will still help you get the "best deal" by showing you how to deal with your choice.

Here are a few suggestions to help you choose the right dealership:

Contact your local Better Business Bureau. If a division does not exist in your area, there is always some kind of consumer protection or reporting agency available to the general public. Call them up and ask them if they can tell you anything about the car dealership you're considering.

Dealer stickers. Almost all dealerships put a sticker or a plate with its name on the vehicles it sells. If you don't have friends or family who have bought from the dealership that you are considering, ask a stranger. You will be surprised at how willing people are to offer information about their purchase and service experiences with a car dealership.

Location. Make sure that a dealership is convenient and that its sales and service hours meet your needs.

C.S.I. (Customer Satisfaction Index). Attempt to check out a dealership's C.S.I. rating, which is explained in the next section.

Visit. Visit a few dealerships before you decide where you want to shop. Browse, listen and watch how it deals with its customers. Like meeting people, your first impression is usually the right one.

What is C.S.I. (Customer Satisfaction Index), and what can it do for you?

Not all programs are called C.S.I., but they are all similar in how they work. C.S.I., which stands for Customer Satisfaction Index, is a report card on dealerships and salespeople. It was developed because automobile manufacturers wanted an unbiased way to find out how their dealerships took care of their customers. The best way was to survey customers themselves. With most rating programs, customers who have just purchased a vehicle will receive a survey at the first, third, sixth, ninth, 12th and 24th month after their purchase date. Unfortunately, less than half of such surveys are filled out and actually returned.

The fact that the customer rates the dealership is what makes the information so important and valuable. Those of you who have bought a new vehicle are aware of these surveys. What you may not be aware of is how they can be used to help you get the "best deal."

> *It is important to complete these surveys and send them in. You will be doing yourself, and future buyers, a great service. Today, many dealerships use these surveys as a part of their selling process. The greater the percentage of customers of any given dealership that respond to these questionnaires, the more realistic a picture can be drawn about how a dealership actually takes care of its customers.*

Few salespeople volunteer to show C.S.I. information on their own because not every dealership can be rated the best. They fear that the consumer may choose any dealership that is rated above them, regardless of convenience as a consideration. When you request to see ratings reports, let the dealership know that you are looking to buy from it and that you simply want to make sure that it deserves your business. This approach will usually get you the information you are looking for.

At the very least, these reports usually include a dealership's ratings on the following services, based on the answers supplied by previous customers:

Sales and management treatment. The survey will ask you about your specific experience with a dealership's sales and management personnel. They will ask how helpful they were, how extensive their product knowledge was and if your vehicle's operating procedures and options were thoroughly explained. Have you heard from your salesperson and dealership since you made your purchase? These questions, along with many others, are designed to grade your overall experience with the dealership.

Vehicle preparation. Was the vehicle ready on time? Was everything working properly? Was it clean?

Service. Attitude, quality, appearance, readiness, price, convenience, availability of loaners or rentals and so on.

Recommendations. About the dealer, salespeople, management, service, the vehicle, the manufacturer and so on.

All of this information is sent back to the manufacturer, which compiles a report on all your responses, good or bad, and sends the results back to the dealership and the individual salesperson. These reports also include a comparison of how dealerships in a district rate against each other.

By requesting that the dealership show you its C.S.I. reports, you can get a firsthand look at the experiences of its previous customers. Some dealerships will not show them to you at all, while some will show you only a part of them. In many cases, they will not show you how they compare to other local dealerships, but they may show you the areas of doing business in which they rated well. The same kind of surveys and reports are made on salespeople. Ask yours to show his or hers to you. Even if he or she has changed dealerships, as long as he or she is with the same brand of dealership, the reports will follow. Who can give you this information? Your salesperson or any department manager usually has a copy of the dealership's individual reports.

Ratings reports are not necessarily meant to be viewed by the public, and the dealership has no obligation to show them to you. However, it has been my experience that dealerships that have rated well with their customers are willing to make the results available. (You may wish to inform the dealership that you are not interested whether it is rated #1, just whether its rating is good enough to earn your business.)

Checking out a dealership's service department

Although you hope that the vehicle you have chosen is going to be reliable, remember that automobiles are machines, and even those with the best reputations can have problems. Whether for routine maintenance or not, you will most likely spend a lot more time with a dealership's service department than you did with its sales department.

AutoSave Tip

When I was a salesperson, many consumers asked me about the quality of the service department at my dealership. I don't think you need to think very long before realizing that a salesperson is not the person to ask about the service department. What do you think he or she is going to tell you? On the other hand, if you ask the salesperson about how reliable the service department is and *then* ask him or her to back up claims with something in writing or with any awards the service department may have won, we're talking about a whole new question.

These are some of the ways that you can judge a dealership's service:

1. Check out its C.S.I. reports.

2. Ask about the dealership's service department when you call the Better Business Bureau.

3. Visit the service department. The best time is in the early morning or late afternoon when customers are dropping off or picking up their vehicles. This is the best way to get first-hand information on how customers are treated. You'll also see whether the department is adequately staffed to handle its volume of business.

4. Inquire about the availability of loaner or rental cars or any kind of services to get you to and from the dealership while your vehicle is being taken care of.

5. Inquire about service hours. Many dealerships offer you the ability to drop off and pick up your vehicle during non business hours. Good dealerships will offer flexibility to help meet the needs of their customers.

6. Ask about any special training or qualifications a dealership's mechanics may have. Some dealerships invest a lot of money in mechanics and their equipment. This type of dealerhip can truly add to your level of satisfaction.

7. Ask if there is a customer relations representative. A frequent complaint that many people have is trying to find someone who has the time or is willing to help them with a problem. Better dealerships will invest in this position.

As with anything and everything, nothing is 100 percent! The same holds true with service departments. Even if a dealership had a 90 percent total satisfaction rate with its service customers, if that dealership is working on 100 cars per day, that would mean 10 people everyday are dissatisfied. Like any gamble, you need to go with the odds. Hopefully you will end up falling on the right side of the fence.

Shopping dealerships over the telephone

The first comment I would like to make is that you can't buy a vehicle over the phone! I'm not saying that using the telephone is not a good thing to do. I'm just saying that I have yet to meet anyone who knew how to shop over the phone. Every day consumers call dealerships asking for prices and even telling the salesperson that they intend to call other dealerships for prices too. If you were one of those individuals, or have been thinking about becoming one, stop wasting your time!

Within the industry, customers who shop by phone are referred to as "phone-ups." On average, dealerships receive as many phone-ups in a day as they get people walking in the door. Knowing that, don't you think salespeople have been trained to handle people on the phone? I can say a lot about telephone shopping, but this is one instance in which I am going to stand up for automobile salespeople and ask you to stop driving them crazy with the telephone!

Here are the only reasons you should use the telephone in your shopping process:

1. To find out if a dealership has a particular vehicle in stock. (Even this can be a waste of time because many salespeople are trained to always say yes. They can later use the excuse that the vehicle was sold just before you got there.)

2. To find out the hours of the dealership and to make an appointment with a particular salesperson.

3. If you do insist on shopping price over the phone, the only question you should be asking is for how much over invoice the dealership is willing to sell the particular model you are considering.

As discussed in the section on low-balling on page 83, it is much easier for a salesperson to lie to someone when they are not face to face. Remember that there should no longer be a fear of negotiating, or of being taken advantage of, if you have been following the guidelines that I have been offering you.

Summary

As I have already repeated numerous times, the reliability and reputation of whom you do business with are going to be the key factors to your overall satisfaction. With very little effort, you ought to be able to find a dealership that you want to do business with. Don't fall into the typical consumer shopping habit of going from dealership to dealership asking what its best price is and deciding who you are going to buy from based on the lowest price you find. You may think that you are doing yourself a favor, but believe me, you're not! What, then, are the new rules you should have learned here?

1. There are plenty of tools available to you for checking out the quality of a dealership.

2. Never take a salesperson's word for anything. If he or she makes a claim, ask him or her to back it up with something in writing.

3. Don't use the telephone for any other reasons than I mentioned.

I chose to name this chapter "First things first" because there are a number of things that you should be doing before you even start to shop. In this chapter, I have discussed how to start preparing yourself for the shopping experience, what is the right vehicle, how to establish your budget, what to do about your current vehicle and how to choose the right dealership. If, and only if, you understand and have actually completed each one of the steps that I just mentioned, are you ready to move on to Chapter 3.

You are ready if you have completed *all* of the following steps:

1. You have created your shopping list and you know exactly what you want and/or require in the vehicle you are going to purchase.

2. You have narrowed your choices down to no more than two or three vehicles, one of which is going to be the vehicle that you will buy.

3. You have established an exact budget for yourself that includes all of the considerations that were discussed in this chapter.

4. You have researched and determined the value of your current vehicle and have decided whether you are going to trade it in or sell it on your own.

5. You have checked out your local dealerships and have decided from whom you are going to make your purchase.

If you have completed all of these steps, then let's go shopping!

Chapter 3

Let's go shopping

Automotive advertising

Based on the information I have given you thus far, you should have no need for paying attention to automotive advertising, other than to learn about a current incentive program an automobile manufacturer is offering or to receive an introduction to a new model. You should be using the techniques I have shown you to determine, on your own, how much you intend to pay for a vehicle, what vehicle you are going to purchase and from whom you are going to purchase it.

Now that I have gotten that out of the way, I will state that I do recognize the importance of understanding automotive advertising, and for very good reasons. Our buying habits are often influenced by holidays and gimmicks. The advertising industry and its clients have always made use of this fact, and probably always will. The important thing to recognize is that just because a president is having a birthday, a season is changing or a dealership puts out red tags, has a giant gorilla on its roof or uses any other gimmick, it will make little or no difference in the deal you can make on your purchase! The dealership's cost doesn't suddenly change just because a promotion is on.

Advertising, as well as most dealership sales tactics, helps to propagate the notion that "price" is the main concern when buying a vehicle. It attempts to lead the consumer's focus away from the "best deal" as I have previously described it. And just in case you have forgotten, the "best deal" is service, convenience and price—and, most importantly, in that order.

With today's level of competition, the advertising of vehicles has become more complex. Monthly payments for purchases or leases are often shown with half of the advertisement consisting of conditions or disclaimers. The only way I have been able to read most automobile advertisements on television has been by using the freeze-frame function on my VCR. With print ads, as well, most consumers only skim the big print, and an asterisk is often used to refer to an area of small print that is supposed to explain the conditions or disclaimers. The problem is that these conditions or disclaimers are worded in a way that few consumers understand. In fact, in many cases, the wording is so confusing that even the salespeople often have a difficult time understanding it.

AutoSave Tip

Do not rely on advertising as a buying tool. It should be used only to view a product, get an idea of its price range or learn about current incentive programs.

Automobile advertising can be separated into two segments: manufacturer to consumer and dealership to consumer. The primary objective of both is to get you into the showroom, where *salespeople* will then take care of you.

Manufacturer's advertising. The manufacturer is dealing with the entire country as its market. Its ads are typically more straightforward, primarily giving you information about its company, products or current incentive programs. Until recently, most manufacturers' ads showed only the base price of a vehicle. As many consumers learned, it was usually a far cry from an actual buying price. A recent deception has been advertising conditional monthly payments, with the conditions often being incentive programs not available to everyone. More can be read in the section "Incentive programs and factory orders" on page 74.

Dealership or dealership group advertising. The dealership has a much more confined market area. Unlike national advertising, the laws involved with local ads can vary greatly from state to state and even by town. Unfortunately for the consumer, this often gives the local dealerships much more leeway in how creative or misleading their advertising can be.

Another form of automotive advertising is done by way of "dealer referral services." This topic is discussed in the section "The choice is yours" on page 64.

I could write an entire book about the types of deceptive advertising I have seen car dealerships use. The problem is, an attempt to write about all of these ads would not only make things more confusing to most consumers, it would go against my belief that the best policy is simply to steer clear of automotive advertising altogether. Here are a few examples of why automotive advertising can be so confusing and why you should not rely on it:

---

1. Package discounts are offered on most vehicles. Most advertising laws allow dealerships to add the amount of these package discounts back onto the M.S.R.P. of the vehicle. This allows the dealership to advertise an inflated list price, then show an inflated discount—the package discount to which you were already entitled.

2. In ads for lease payments, the fine print often includes the mention of a C.R., or cap reduction. A cap reduction is actually a down payment. This is an example of the use of alternate, legitimate terms that salespeople understand but few consumers recognize.

3. "If qualified" can be the most misleading ad disclaimer of all. One hundred percent financing "if qualified" usually means for homeowners only, with AAA credit, who may have to put up their homes as collateral for the loan. The advertising of rebates "if qualified" is used to show lower selling prices in big print. Many of these rebates are only for a specific segment of the public, such as a "first-time buyer," "business owner," recent "college graduate" and so on. If you don't happen to fall within this small segment of individuals who qualify for these rebates, then the advertised price is not what you will have to pay!

4. I once viewed a television ad in which a multi-franchise dealership claimed to offer $4,000 for any trade-in that you could drive or push into its lot. Half of the screen was a disclaimer shown for only a few seconds. In other words, the disclaimer, like most, was almost impossible to read. The ad then listed all of the different makes the dealership sold. It really sounded great, especially to people who had old junks for which other dealerships offered them next to nothing. It wasn't until I used the freeze-frame function on my VCR that I discovered that the disclaimer stated that the offer was good only on the purchase of a new "customized" van, also known as a conversion van. Since the automobile manufacturers do not produce the customized vans themselves, the "asking price," or supposed M.S.R.P., is any amount the dealership wants it to be. These customized vans are often marked up $5,000 to $10,000 above dealer cost. Based on

the disclaimer in that ad, the dealership could have offered a $4,000 trade-in value for a pencil. Needless to say, the ad did its job, and the showroom was soon packed with potential customers.

5. Another recent advertising craze is to state that "all credit applications will be accepted!" This sounds great, especially if you happen to have questionable credit. Of course, once again, the ad is simply making use of words—or in this case, a word—that the advertiser knows is easily misleading. Did you think of the word "approved" when they really used the word "accepted"? My research has shown that this is the case with most consumers. All this advertisement states is that the dealer will physically accept your application and send it into the bank. The entire ad is an erroneous deception designed to take advantage of consumers.

6. "We will pay off your trade-in no matter how much you owe!" Another great-sounding advertisement that means absolutely nothing. Of course, it's designed to make people think that somehow, during this supposed special deal, the dealership is going to release you from the obligation of any loan or lease balance your trade-in may have. All they are really stating is that they will physically handle the process of paying your trade off. Whatever money you owed will simply be added on to the loan of your new vehicle or subtracted from any equity your vehicle has.

Even if I were to list all of the deceptive ads that I have seen, it wouldn't do you any good. The problem is, just as quickly as these ads are exposed or withdrawn from the media, new and better ones are created.

Summary

If you believe that someone spends thousands of dollars in advertising to give something away, then I have a lot more work cut out for me than I thought. Remember, almost all advertising is based on selling you a "price," and the selling price of a vehicle represents the *least* amount of profit that a dealer makes on the sale of a vehicle.

I highly doubt that misleading advertising will ever get any better. In fact, as competition increases, it will surely get worse, for the consumer that is. You see, even if a dealership wants to advertise legitimately, it can't, because if it does, every other ad out there is going to sound better, and the dealership would just be throwing its money down the proverbial drain.

What, then, are the new rules you should have learned from this section?

1. Don't rely on advertising as a buying tool!
2. Always read the fine print if you feel forced to read the ads!
3. Remember that the only reason for advertising is to get you in the showroom.

Where and when to shop

When should you shop?

There is a lot to be said for timing. The hour of the day, the day of the week, the week of the month and the month of the year can each be a factor in getting your "best deal."

Although I am about to offer you some advice on the best time to shop, the bottom line is that it really shouldn't matter. If you have properly armed yourself with the information I have given you, including knowing dealer cost and choosing the right dealership, then the following information is only offered in the light that these are times when you will find the least amount of resistance to your offer.

Time of day. Car salespeople put in very long hours. Often starting the day at 8 or 9 in the morning, many dealerships stay open until 10 p.m. By dinner time, little is usually thought about except going home. The last couple of hours before closing is the best time to find the least amount of resistance from both the salespeople and sales management, who are often tired and frustrated by a long day.

Day of the week. At the end of the week (Saturday or Sunday, depending on local laws), the sales department is reviewing the past week of business. If it was good, and good paychecks are coming, the salespeople are all more relaxed. If it was bad, they are ready to do just about anything by the weekend to make a deal. In either case you win! Weekends are considered a volume time for business for the dealership. The showroom is usually at its busiest. Less effort will be spent on lengthy and hard-core sales tactics, giving you the opportunity to make a quicker and easier purchase.

AutoSave Tip

The one drawback of the weekend, or any time there is a volume of customers, is that you may run across salespeople who quickly attempt to "qualify" you in regard to how ready you are to make a purchase. Often, phrases such as "Are you ready to buy a vehicle today if the deal is right?" will be used. If your answer is no, salespeople may become very abrupt and offer you little help. This is because they want to move on to a customer who is looking to make a deal on the spot. This situation can be avoided if you follow the suggestions I give in "Choosing the 'right' salesperson," on page 66.

Week of the month. Most salespeople's and managers' pay plans are based on a monthly cycle. However, when it comes to shopping for the "best deal," some weeks of the month are better than others:

- **First week.** Anxious to get a new month off to a good start, the sales crew is generally energetic and ready for anything. The previous end-of-the-month sales meeting, in which they were either praised or beat on, has charged them up. This is not a good week to shop, but it is better than the second and third week.

- **Second and third week.** Now it is time to get down to making a living. The middle of the month is usually when salespeople are concentrating most on their income and in-house incentive programs. I would consider these the worst two weeks of the month to shop.

- **Fourth week.** Regardless of how many sales they have or have not made for the month so far, the last week of each month is considered to be a volume period for sales. Salespeople and managers alike are competing in contests or are concerned with their quotas. Dealership owners themselves are competing for district standings, which are reported on a monthly basis. This last week of the month, especially the last few days, is definitely the best time to shop.

Month of the year. Spring and fall are the two hottest selling seasons. Spring fever brings out the people who have been dreaming all winter of a new vehicle or those who spent the winter having problems with their current one. Fall introduces new models and creates leftovers. Because these are the hottest selling seasons, dealerships and salespeople are usually less willing to negotiate, and manufacturers' incentive programs are usually at their lowest. Summer is basically middle of the road, but winter, being the slowest selling season, usually brings out the best deals and incentive programs. Don't let the idea of buying a new vehicle during bad weather sway you from the opportunity to make a better, easier deal. Leftovers will be cheap, and new models will have yet to get their first price increase.

To sum it up, the best time to negotiate your deal would be in the late fall or winter, a couple of hours before closing and preferably the last weekend of the month.

Where should you shop?

Although the existence of auto malls and large highway dealerships leads us to think otherwise, the fact has already been established that all dealerships pay the same price. You can get a good price anywhere. Getting the "best deal" is what this book is all about.

The location of a dealership can often influence how it does business. A large dealership located in a high traffic area is often able to do business regardless of its reputation. This type of dealership simply sells the concept of price and selection but rarely spends the time or money to offer good service. Its volume of traffic makes it less dependent on repeat business. It often treats the consumer as just a sale, not as a customer, and simply tries to make the most profit any time it may have the opportunity. The salespeople usually have much less training and are the most transient of all salespeople. In other words, they will be of little help to you in making the deal and probably won't be around too long afterwards, either!

AutoSave Tip

Whenever possible, buy from the dealership you are going to use for service! My favorite analogy to express why this is important is: "Whose children would you take care of first and better—yours or a stranger's?" The answer is obvious, and it can usually be applied to how a dealership treats its customers.

An in-town dealership, or a dealership that is at least slightly off the beaten path, depends on its reputation to stay in business. Each customer is looked at as a customer with the potential for repeat sales and referrals. Here you will usually find salespeople who have been there for years. They are often more knowledgeable about their products, are friends with the rest of the dealership personnel and are anxious not only to make you a repeat customer, but hopefully to please you enough that you will refer others. (Refer to "Choosing the 'right' salesperson" on page 66.)

Summary

Regarding when you should shop, the only advantage you may find by using the time tables I offered you is catching dealerships or salespeople when they are the hungriest or at a point of offering the least resistance. Once again, dealer invoice doesn't change (except as previously noted). You can get just as good of a deal regardless of the timing that you choose.

In respect to where to shop, most of the important information was offered in the section "Choosing the 'right' dealership" on page 46 in Chapter 2.

What are the new rules that you should have learned from this section? This section simply added to your knowledge and ability to take control of the shopping and purchasing experience. It is important to realize that the automotive industry attempts to take control by telling you when and where to shop. Only when you are in control are you truly deciding the rules of a winning game plan.

The choice is yours

Dealer referral services

In recent years, many organizations and publications have begun to offer dealer referral and/or price shopping services. The problem I have seen with these services is that many are vague, irresponsible and often both. The organizations or publications that claim to offer special prices rarely check out a dealership's reputation. They act as little more than an advertising promotion. Any dealership willing to pay a fee to be listed will be listed. Many will advertise that you can buy a vehicle for "as little as 1 percent more than dealer invoice." If you read the fine print, you will often find the statement "or up to 10 percent over invoice" and that not all models are included. This basically tells consumers that they will pay somewhere between dealer cost and full list price on most vehicles. Even the worst shoppers can make that kind of a deal on their own.

Some organizations do take the time to investigate dealerships, and their services can offer you valuable information about a dealership's reputation. These organization types rarely get involved with offering supposed "special prices," although they will often establish pricing guidelines with the dealerships. They, too, recognize that price should not be the only consideration and are concerned with recommending the "big picture" to their customers.

Credit unions have recently joined the ranks of organizations attempting to offer their members special buying services. They usually make arrangements with dealerships in their area to offer their members vehicles at prices that are a "better" amount, or percentage, over dealer invoice. You can already do this on your own. You don't need their services, and unless they can show you that they have also investigated the reliability and reputation of the dealerships they recommend, you should avoid their offers totally.

Some of the "price" services that are available lead the consumer to believe that they can get a better price from dealerships based on the volume of purchases that such services make for their clients. As previously discussed, volume has little or nothing to do with what kind of price anyone can get. The fact of the matter is, the dealerships or salespeople who participate in these programs are only foregoing some of the intensity that they would normally apply to negotiating. These same dealerships are going to spend as much, if not more, effort in concentrating on their back-end profits. In many cases, your overall purchase price will be higher, and you may end up with a dealership that has poor service or is not conveniently located.

AutoSave Tip

Contact the company offering the dealer referral service. Find out exactly what qualifications, if any, it uses to list a dealership. My experience, in general, is that buying services are simply a waste of your time, and sometimes your money! They offer you nothing more than you are currently learning how to do yourself.

Shopping on the Internet

I doubt too many people can claim to be more of a computer junkie than I am, and when it comes to the Internet, I surf on a regular basis. Still truly in its infancy, the Internet is becoming a marketplace of new strategies for growth in many businesses, and the automotive sales industry is certainly an active participant. Recently, I have been part of a project, gathering information about the buying habits and motives of consumers looking to shop for their vehicles online. More than just a fun and an "intimately private" way of shopping, the "information superhighway" has become just that, a great place to gather information. Is it a great place to buy from? I'm not convinced of that as yet. I would certainly advise using the Internet to gain as much information as possible regarding the vehicle(s) that you are considering. Even finding out how much the dealership paid for them.

But the actual purchase or purchase arrangements of a vehicle are too personal to me. I want to meet who I am thinking about spending my hard-earned money with. I want to see the dealership, check it out, and be able to make a comfortable *emotional* decision, not just a financial one.

Will the Internet probably play a greater role in our automotive purchases in the future? I would venture to state a definitive yes! Will it necessarily make us a more satisfied consumer in the long run? I highly doubt it. As with everything that I have discussed so far, once again, it is important to keep the "big picture" in mind. What am I gaining? And what might I be sacrificing or losing in the process?

Choosing the "right" salesperson

One of the biggest mistakes consumers make is letting the salesperson pick them, instead of picking the salesperson.

Car dealerships usually have one of two systems that determine how a salesperson gets to greet a consumer. One is called the "up" system, in which the salespeople take turns; and the other is an "open floor" system, in which the salesperson who gets you is the one who approached you first. You don't need to and shouldn't be playing by their rules. By the time you are ready to make your "buying" decisions, your needs have become fairly specific. You want a salesperson who has the experience and knowledge to help you with your personal buying needs and the stability of someone who will hopefully be there in the future.

The best way to choose a salesperson is to be referred to him or her. If you know anyone who has made a purchase from the dealership you are considering, ask about his or her salesperson. One thing I know for certain, a salesperson will treat a referral with more respect. A salesperson who has earned the right to be referred is usually one who is stable and is looking for your repeat and referral business. He or she will generally deal with you on a more honest basis. If a salesperson doesn't know an answer to your question, he or she is more likely to learn it, rather than guess or lie.

Choosing the right salesperson will do more towards making your shopping and purchasing experience more fun and rewarding than almost anything else will!

AutoSave Tip

If you're not referred to a salesperson, see the sales manager when you enter the dealership. Tell him or her that you want to be introduced to someone who is experienced with your specific needs and has been with the dealership for at least a couple of years. Tell him or her what your specific needs are, such as buying a truck or leasing. Few salespeople know all the aspects of the business. By approaching management first, you are more likely to meet a salesperson who is qualified to help you. A side benefit to this is that you have already put management on your side. Starting from the top will be a tremendous asset to how you are treated, along with how easily you are able to get the "best deal."

Summary

The point I tried to make in this section was that you have choices. Don't let people and businesses tell you what you can and cannot—or should and should not—do.

I believe that dealer referral services have sprung out of the frustrations of consumers who were afraid of being taken advantage of—who thought that maybe by using these services, they could leave a dealership without wondering whether they made a good deal.

I have occasionally, very occasionally, been surprised by seeing customers tell a salesperson that they did not like him or her, and that they wanted to speak with someone else. Most consumer's feel that they are stuck with whomever "got" them when they pulled into the lot. This, of course, as you have just read, is not the case. What new rules should you have learned from this section?

1. Don't utilize dealer referral services. They don't offer anything you can't do on your own and, in fact, often offer less.

2. Always choose your salesperson! It starts the relationship off with *you* in control instead of the salesperson!

3. The Internet can be a great place to gather information, but not necessarily to make an actual purchase.

Understanding window stickers

What are Monroney labels?

The term "Monroney label," named for the Congressman who initiated its use, refers to the actual manufacturer's window sticker on all new vehicles. It is required by law to be on the vehicle or that vehicle cannot be offered for sale. It gives you the following information:

- **The year, make and model** designation of the vehicle.

- **Standard equipment.** Usually shown on the left side of the label, the equipment shown is what comes standard from the factory and it represents the base sticker price before options.

- **Options.** Options are listed in two ways. Individual ones are shown with their prices. Option packages show the full list of options with one sum price for all of them. A figure showing the "package discount" is usually listed below this sum.

- **Engine and transmission.** This will often be shown twice on the window sticker—once in the standard equipment area and again in the options area. The two listings may differ if the vehicle was ordered with an engine or transmission that is not standard equipment.

- **Fuel economy.** Shows the average "city" and "highway" fuel economy of the vehicle along with two other ratings—an average spread and a model comparison rating, which are explained in more detail in "Fuel economy ratings" on page 72.

- **Manufacturer's Suggested Retail Price (M.S.R.P.)** is shown in two areas—first, before the listed options (this represents the M.S.R.P. of the base vehicle) and second, after the list of options (this represents the M.S.R.P. of the vehicle as it is currently equipped). It is important to note the M.S.R.P. cannot, and will not, vary from dealer to dealer. If the vehicles are equipped the same way, the M.S.R.P. will be exactly the same. The only times there can be a variation is if one vehicle happened to be a "pre-price increase" unit or if shipping fees (freight) vary in different states, or different marketing strategies are used for different states (see following note).

Each automobile manufacturer breaks down marketing strategies into "selling regions" throughout the country. Their regional offices often package vehicles differently based on the needs or wants of the consumers in their area. They can create "regional package incentives." For instance, in the northeast region of the United States, because of its concentration of large cities, most customers may want an automatic transmission. Based on this, manufacturers may create a special regional incentive program that offers the automatic for free. With this form of regional marketing and incentives, it is possible to find vehicles in different states that may be equipped the same but have a different M.S.R.P.

• **Origin.** the city in which the vehicle was built, will be shown at the bottom of the label. Inside the driver's side door jamb will be another label showing the manufacturer that built the vehicle and where it was built.

Monroney labels can be a bit confusing. If their information is not clear to you, have the salesperson explain it.

Are "package discounts" for real?

Basically, we have the import vehicle manufacturers to thank for the "package" concept. Because the factories are too far away to allow for individualized orders, they had to develop a different approach to marketing their products in the U.S. The most basic approach was to create different levels of option packages under which each model would be sold. Today, most import vehicle models are designated as either Standard (S), Deluxe (DX), Luxury (LX) or Grand Touring (GT).

Domestic manufacturers recognized that one of the benefits to this form of marketing was the ability to streamline production. Packaging options greatly improved the assembly process. Because that lowered their costs in a highly competitive market, part of those savings could be passed on to the consumer.

Many consumers believe that package discounts are simply the product of inflated option prices. I sold vehicles during the domestic market's transition to the package concept, and I saw no unusual changes in individual option pricing. More efficient production has offered the consumer the new benefit of the package discount.

As previously mentioned, the window sticker will usually show what you might be led to believe are two M.S.R.P. prices—the first one being the list price of the vehicle before any package discounts, and the second one, at the bottom of the sticker, being the M.S.R.P. of the vehicle after package discounts. Many dealerships make use of package discounts in their advertising and selling techniques. For example, they may advertise a vehicle's original list price of $11,400 in big print and then show, in small print, the package discount of $500 added to their discount of $1,500—then, back in large print again, show a $2,000 discount. This is flat-out deception. The actual M.S.R.P. of the vehicle is $10,900—$11,400 minus the package discount of $500. They are offering you a dealer discount of only $1,500.

This technique is also often used during "red tag" sales, sales in which a red tag may show in large print a discount of $3,000, a part of which is comprised of the package discount to which you are already entitled. Salespeople, especially, like to list the inflated figure, the one before the package discount, when they fill out their worksheets to start negotiating with you. They know that many consumers seem more concerned with how much of a discount they perceive they are getting, rather than how much they are actually paying for the vehicle. The bottom line here, regardless of the scenario, is to make sure you are dealing with the actual M.S.R.P. of a vehicle—the amount listed at the very bottom of the window sticker.

Dealer "add-on" labels

An "add-on" label is a charge the dealerships adds on to the price of a vehicle in addition to the original manufacturer's window sticker. There are two primary reasons why dealerships may add these to a vehicle; behind both reasons is a desire to increase their profits.

1. **Availability.** When demand is greater than supply, someone is going to try to make extra money. More so with imports, some vehicles are simply hard to get. Dealerships will often use add-on labels to get a premium for these vehicles, using terms such as "market availability," "acquisition fee" or any other term to justify an additional charge. I have seen these labels range from $200 to $20,000. This is usually all net profit for the dealership.

Availability fees will usually decrease or stop over time. A good example is the limited-production ZR1 Corvette. Some consumers paid up to $20,000 more than M.S.R.P. when it was introduced. Less than a year later, the car could be bought for less than M.S.R.P. If a limited edition vehicle sells well, production will usually bo incroasod. A short wait could save you a lot of money.

2. **Profit margin.** Some basic vehicles have only a few hundred dollars markup between invoice and full retail, leaving little room for negotiating. Others, as explained above, may be hard to get (at times, because of nothing more than a popular color) but are not really limited production. In addition to or in place of market availability fees, dealerships will often add options to a vehicle of this type to help increase its selling price and potential for profits. These options, ranging from pin-striping to power sunroofs, are always marked up at a very high profit margin. Some are simply used to enhance a plain vehicle and make it easier to sell.

AutoSave Tip

Market availability or dealer add-ons are rarely reflected in the resale value of your vehicle. Regardless of how much extra you've paid, most or all of this will be a total loss to you at resale or trade-in.

Dealer "add-on" labels are also used for customized vehicles. A dealership may send a regular cargo van to a van conversion company and have all sorts of work done to it. By the time it comes back, it may resemble a "living room on wheels" more than a van. A dealership then has the ability to place an add-on label on that vehicle and select any suggested retail price markup that it thinks the market will bear.

This practice is also common for trucks. Light-duty dump trucks are not built by automobile manufacturers. The dealership receives only what is known as a cab and chassis. The cab and chassis are sent to a body company to have any of a wide variety of bodies placed on the chassis. Once again, the dealership has the opportunity to inflate its markup by any amount that it chooses based on the cost of the body. For example, let's say the dump body the dealership chose to put on the cab and chassis cost $4,000. The dealership may mark up the price on the cab and chassis with an add-on label showing a new M.S.R.P. that is $8,000 higher than the cab and chassis would have been on its own.

Of course a dealership doesn't want to price itself out of the market, but the most basic rule of selling is that you can come down in price a lot easier than you can go up. Once again, dealerships know that consumers like to see big discounts, even if those discounts are actually being given from a highly inflated list price.

Fuel economy ratings

Since the early 1980s, the window sticker listing of fuel economy ratings has changed. Prior to this time, fuel economy was listed as the "best" fuel economy a vehicle could achieve in either city or highway conditions. Many consumers were upset with these figures because they were usually unrealistic, except under the most perfect driving conditions. Today, the m.p.g. (miles per gallon) of a vehicle is rated as an average, meaning that what you see on the Monroney label is not only realistic, but in many cases, can be exceeded. This, of course, will depend on where you live and how you drive. For example, if you live in a mountainous area, don't expect much, but if you live in a flat country area, your mileage will almost always exceed the ratings.

In addition to listing average city and highway m.p.g., an average spread is listed with a model comparison rating. This rating compares the fuel economy of that particular vehicle with other vehicles in the same size classification. For example, the large numbers on the window sticker may show 17 m.p.g. city and 26 m.p.g. highway. Below that, the sticker may show 14 to 20 city and 23 to 29 highway. This is just a breakdown to help compensate for driving conditions and habits. To the right of these numbers are the model comparison ratings, in which all vehicles are rated according to their size or grouping. The most common sizes or groupings are sub-compact, compact, mid-size, full-size and utility.

The regulations that require the m.p.g. of a vehicle to be shown on the vehicle's Monroney label are applicable only to vehicles that have a G.V.W.R. (Gross Vehicle Weight Rating) of 8,500 pounds or less. This is because any vehicle over that weight is surely going to be a commercial truck, and the uses and applications of commercial trucks vary too much to offer a fuel economy rating that would have any meaning.

What is C.A.F.E.?

Corporate Average Fuel Economy (C.A.F.E.) is a government regulation, enforced by the Environmental Protection Agency (E.P.A.), that affects all vehicles sold in the United States having a G.V.W. (Gross Vehicle Weight) less than 8,500 pounds. This regulation was designed to enforce a fuel economy standard for the total sales of a manufacturer each year. If the standard in any given year is not met, the manufacturer must pay a fine of $5 per vehicle sold for each one-tenth deviation from the standard m.p.g. (fine rate based on 1991 figures). For example, if a manufacturer failed to meet the 1991 passenger car standard of 27.5 m.p.g. by one mile per gallon, and it sold one million vehicles, the penalty would have been $5.00 x 10 x 1 million, which would have equaled a fine of $50,000,000.

How does C.A.F.E. affect us? Basically, C.A.F.E. is there to ensure energy conservation. It has forced automobile manufacturers to research and develop more fuel-efficient systems. The consumer is the pays the final bill for R&D, but today's automobiles have doubled the average m.p.g. from just a couple of decades ago.

C.A.F.E. can create availability problems. If a manufacturer has not had a good year selling highly fuel-efficient vehicles, it may intentionally reduce the availability of the more powerful engines used in its sports cars, luxury cars and trucks in order to avoid a poor fuel economy rating. The fines are generally higher than is worth the sale of a few extra vehicles. As previously discussed, availability will often affect the price that you have to pay for the vehicle. This is why some high-end sport and luxury cars have a gas-guzzler tax on their window stickers, which is added to their price. The manufacturer may build them, but you will pay the fines.

Sometimes there is an added benefit to these regulations. An automobile or truck manufacturer may offer special incentives on vehicles having a manual transmission, which would offer a higher fuel economy rating. Free air conditioning on a truck with a manual transmission is just one example of special incentives that consumers may be able to take advantage of.

Summary

The purpose of this section was to educate you about the window stickers that both the automobile manufacturers and the dealerships place on their vehicles. Hopefully, it also gave you a little insight into how fuel economy ratings work and an understanding of the E.P.A.'s role in the automotive business.

What, then, are the new rules you should have learned from this section? In this case, only one: Be leery of any window sticker that is not the original one from the manufacturer. Any other sticker has no guidelines and may be used to mark up the vehicle with any level of profit the dealership desires. Once again, you should always be working from dealer cost up, not list price down. If something has been added to a vehicle, ask the salesperson to show you the invoice showing how much the dealership paid for the item!

Incentive programs and factory orders

Understanding incentive programs

There are two basic types of incentive programs: manufacturer to dealership and manufacturer to consumer. They are generally in the form of a rebate, interest rate, lease rate or a combination of each. Few actually affect a dealership's cost. Those that do are usually graduated level programs in which the rebate increases as the dealership sells more vehicles. Although this type is the least common, ask what type of rebate you are being offered. If it is a graduated level program, waiting an extra week or two may save you hundreds of extra dollars.

Many consumers complain that "incentive programs" have gotten out of hand. What once was a simple rebate or low interest rate is now often so confusing that even many car salespeople have a hard time understanding it. The list of conditions just seems to go on and on. Take the rebate and you don't get the special interest rate, or vice versa. Only certain models apply. Only certain people can have the incentive. College rebates, business rebates, equipment rebates, etc. The question many consumers ask is, "Why don't they just lower the price of the vehicle itself?"

Because many of these programs are specific to a particular model or buying segment of the public, if the manufacturers simply reduced the price, everyone would save. This is not their intention. It is often just a means to pick up on business they normally might not have had. They still need full retail sales to maintain profit levels.

AutoSave Tip

Consumers are often unaware of the incentive programs available. Always ask your salesperson what programs you or your vehicle might be eligible for. Maybe you usually pay cash. If a previous auto loan doesn't show up on your credit report, you may be eligible for a "first-time-buyer rebate." If you recently graduated from college, or will be graduating soon, you may be eligible for a college graduate program.

Let's take a look at some of the basic reasons incentive programs are offered.

Competition. Manufacturers are always battling over who can claim "truck leadership," "best-selling car in America" or other powerful titles that can be used in advertising. Even their best-selling vehicles may be offered with consumer or dealer incentives if the battle for leadership is close. In fact, sometimes the consumer incentives are so strong the vehicle is sold at a loss, in return for the manufacturer being able to gain leadership in advertising power. These incentives are usually seen during the last quarter of a given model year, typically in August, September and October.

Seasons. Many vehicles are seasonal. Sports cars and convertibles certainly need little help being sold in the spring or summer; the same holds true for four-wheel drive vehicles in the winter. Many programs are simply there to help dealerships' off-season sales. In the fall, dealerships are looking for help in getting rid of their leftovers and in introducing the new models.

Fuel economy. As explained in the previous section, C.A.F.E. can affect the number of large or high-performance vehicles a manufacturer can sell. Manufacturers may offer an incentive on high m.p.g. vehicles just so they can sell more of their luxury, sport or full-size truck models.

The important things to watch for with incentives are when and how they apply. Most are designed to get the consumer to buy out of dealership stock. Be sure that you know their rules, especially if you choose to order a vehicle or have one located for you.

Dealer "locates" and "factory orders"

Computer technology has given most dealerships the ability to check the inventory of all their neighboring dealerships through a "locate system." In fact, this system can show inventory pretty much throughout the country, although a dealership is certainly going to look only locally for you. Because of locate systems—unless you really have a need for something unique—placing a factory order rarely needs to be a consideration.

Dealer "locates," or dealer "swaps," as they are referred to inside the industry, are commonplace. The cost of inventorying vehicles has risen to the point that most dealerships have chosen to cooperate with each other rather than simply look at each other as competitors. A dealership does not even need a computer to locate a vehicle for you. All it needs is a telephone and a little effort. However, with the computer system, it can simply enter the model, color and options to get a printout of all the dealerships that have that vehicle in stock.

Once the vehicle is located, the dealership can arrange to swap one of its own vehicles for it. You should not be charged for this service. It is provided as a means to help eliminate factory orders and to provide a quicker turnover of inventory for the dealership.

Because locates take some time and effort, most dealerships will require you to first sign a sales contract and leave a deposit. This is not a problem as long as you do the following.

1. Specify the exact factory options that you want right down to the color. Make it clear and put it in writing that you have the right to a full refund of your deposit if the dealership does not produce the exact vehicle that you agreed upon. You can always offer flexibility later. If the dealership finds a vehicle that is at least close to what you wanted, you can use your ability to be flexible as an additional negotiating tool.

2. Establish a time limit in writing. A locate should take no more than two working days. It is possible that it may take a day or two longer to actually get the vehicle, but within two days the dealership should supply you with a serial number. Include the right to a full refund of your deposit if the dealership doesn't meet these terms.

It is possible that exactly what you want may not exist. If you choose to accept a vehicle that has additional equipment, be certain that you pay only dealer invoice for any extras. Ask to see the dealer invoice.

AutoSave Tip

Low-balling can easily be used with "locates." The dealership can say it has found your vehicle but claim that it has extras—usually those items such as rustproofing, door-edge guards, pinstripes or anything else to raise the price. Of course, you can pass on the vehicle, but typically, the longer a customer waits, the more likely he or she is to compromise. One way to see if these extras are just part of a low-ball is to find out if the dealership is willing to include the items at its own cost. Because an actual invoice may not be available for these dealer-installed options, start your offer at only 25 percent of the price the dealership wants to charge you.

The risks with placing a "factory order"

Incentives. Most incentive programs have time limits, and a program that was in effect at the time you placed your factory order may not apply by the time your order comes in. The terms of incentive programs should be fully explained.

Whether or not a vehicle had an incentive program at the time you placed the order, you, the consumer, are entitled to any program that is in effect at the time you take delivery. Be sure to check on this before you pay for your vehicle. Many dealerships attempt to keep these incentives to themselves, hoping that you are not aware of them because they were not in effect when you placed the original order.

Trade-ins. The back of most sales contracts will include a section about trade-ins that gives the dealership the right to reappraise your trade when the factory order comes in. In essence, this gives the dealership the opportunity to change the original deal that you made. This is sometimes part of a low-ball. Make sure that you have the right to take your trade out of the deal any time prior to delivery of your new vehicle. This may give you the opportunity to retail it on your own. Some dealerships are willing to "future" your trade. This means they agree in writing not to reappraise your trade when your factory order arrives. This does not apply if the condition of your trade-in has changed.

AutoSave Tip

Make sure that actual, not inflated, figures are used on your sales contract. For example, if you were ordering an $18,000 vehicle for which you negotiated a $2,000 discount, and you have a trade that is actually worth $5,000, the order can either be written as $18,000 for the new vehicle and $7,000 for the trade, or as $16,000 for the new vehicle and $5,000 for the trade. In either case, the deal nets out to an $11,000 difference. However, if the sales contract was written the first way and you decide to pull the trade out from the deal, a problem arises: The dealer would have a contract showing that you agreed to pay $18,000 for the new vehicle.

Interest rates. With an ever-changing economy, few banks offer rate protection with a factory order even if your credit application was approved before the order was placed. This, of course, can work both ways. If the bank rates are higher when the vehicle comes in, you will have to pay the higher rate, but if the rates have gone down, you are entitled to the lower rate.

Price increases. Manufacturers that accept factory orders will usually give the consumer price protection. In the event that your order is not protected, you do have the right to cancel. The back of most sales contracts will explain your rights in more detail.

The time it takes your order to arrive. If a dealership believes it can get your business by offering a shorter delivery time than its competitor, it may low-ball the time. The dealership is aware that if it takes longer than is promised, you probably will not cancel your order. Doing so would mean that you would have to start all over again with another dealership. There is, in fact, no way for a dealership to guarantee how long a factory order will take. Variables can include production cycles, holidays, strikes and numerous other factors that can delay delivery. Most factory orders should arrive in four to eight weeks. A dealership is notified regularly by the manufacturer of the status of all vehicles it has on order. This will usually include an estimated time of arrival. Tell your salesperson that you want to be kept up-to-date about the status of your order. Printouts are usually sent to the dealer once a week, but the dealership's own computer can usually give daily status reports.

AutoSave Tip

Contact the manufacturer's local district sales office if you think a vehicle is taking too long. This office can often help to speed up the process or inform you of a production problem that the dealership might not have told you about.

Factory orders and imports. I know of no import manufacturer that allows you to place a factory order. Import dealerships work with an allocation system. The dealership has little, if anything, to say about what vehicles it receives. With import dealerships, an order is usually nothing more than being put on a "waiting list." (Based on a written order, some import manufacturers will allow a dealership to do a little picking and choosing from the inventory at the port). Question your dealership about how it intends to fill your order and be sure to always include a time limit if you place one.

Unless you are actually purchasing from a dealership's advanced allocation notice, do not simply be put on a waiting list. This is a popular way for import dealerships to low-ball customers. They keep you waiting while attempting to sell you something else at a profit level that they really wanted in the first place. Another problem with a waiting list is being passed over. If a dealership has a backlog of orders for a particular model, even a particular color, it may choose who gets it first based solely on how much they paid for it.

Summary

The first thing to understand about incentive programs is that they are almost always available. You should also understand that these programs are offered by the automobile manufacturer, not the dealership. In almost all cases, these programs cost the dealership nothing.

In the event that the dealership does not have the vehicle you want, the key issue here is to realize that very rarely should you have to place a factory order. Make sure the dealership puts forth the effort it should in finding the vehicle you want.

What new rules should you have learned from this section?

1. Don't wait for a salesperson to volunteer information on incentive programs for a particular vehicle. Simply ask if there is any program for your vehicle for which you might qualify.
2. You don't have to settle for what a dealership has on its lot. Because locates require some effort, a salesperson will often try to sell you on the idea that if you don't pick from what is there, your only alternative is to wait X number of weeks for a factory order to come in. Of course, this is rarely true.
3. If you do place an order for a vehicle, make sure that you clearly understand what that means in terms of current interest rates, incentive programs and so on.

Making negotiating easy

The key to making negotiating easy is knowing exactly what you are negotiating for. If the foundation of *buying* something instead of being *sold* something is combined with looking at your purchase with the "big picture" in mind, then negotiating will be easy!

Mostly, the salesperson's job is to get your deposit. Dealerships know that most of their profits are not made on the vehicle itself. What happens is that you find yourself negotiating many different parts of the deal, often after you have already made a commitment to the vehicle. If you use your shopping list, you can negotiate the whole deal at once or at least know exactly what items you do want when the dealership starts its back-end selling process. Nothing should be left to impulse.

AutoSave Tip

One of the most important tips I can offer about negotiating a vehicle's price is that you should be negotiating from the dealer invoice up, not from the list price down. Your first offer should be no more than $200 to $500 more than invoice. As previously mentioned, there are numerous publications and organizations that can supply you with dealer invoice, often for free or just a nominal charge.

When negotiating with two different dealerships, you must be sure that you are comparing two identical products. While most vehicles sold today have "option groups," the extras that a dealership may choose for its inventory often vary. You should request a copy of the window sticker or the dealership's invoice. This will give you an exact listing of all the options that the vehicle has, instead of trying to leave it to memory or jotting down notes.

Years ago, dealerships were often willing to show customers the invoices on the vehicles that they were considering. Unfortunately, consumers became very leery of this practice because of a few bad apples who got the bright idea to manufacture their own fabricated invoices. Today, few, if any, dealerships will jeopardize their licenses to attempt this type of deception. Besides, if you have used the information I gave you in the section on choosing the right dealership, you have basically eliminated doing business with anyone who would still participate in such a scam. You should always ask to see the dealer invoice on a vehicle. It is a lot easier, cheaper and more accurate than trying to use some type of pricing service or publication.

AutoSave Tip

Dealerships sometimes leave out options just to have a price advantage. It is natural for most people to think that a fully equipped vehicle with power windows/locks, cruise control, etc., is going to have a rear defroster. Never take anything for granted. Read the label and inspect the vehicle thoroughly. The omission of easily overlooked options is one way that dealerships can make you think they are offering you a better price than their competitors. Remember, if the M.S.R.P. is not exactly the same, neither are the vehicles.

Documentary fee. Some form of a fee is almost always printed on a dealership's sales order form. In most cases, this fee is nothing more than a way for a dealership to generate additional profits. It, like most everything else, is usually negotiable. If a dealership refuses to negotiate this fee, there may be little that you can actually do about it other than compare the dealership's bottom-line total to that of any other dealership you have also been shopping. Personally, I feel anything more than a $75 documentary fee is outrageous.

Remember, never shop just the price of the vehicle! Be sure to shop the total delivered price. I have seen documentary fees (also referred to as processing fees), computer fees and other terms, range from $35 to $400, while I have also known dealerships and salespeople to inflate the cost of motor vehicle fees. Some dealerships are starting to charge fees just to file your finance application with the bank. Your final price quote should be as if you were ready to hand them the cash and take the vehicle on the spot. It must include everything!

What is a "low-ball"?

As mentioned previously, a "low-ball" is a lie or a deception. It is when you are given a low price for which a dealership has no intention of delivering you a vehicle. Low-balls are used in many parts of the sales process. Let's take a look at a few of them.

Selling price. If salespeople know that you intend to shop, many will often lie about the selling price. More often than not, this "lie" is just a misleading use of words. Phrases such as "What if I could...," "I'll try to get you this price," "I'm sure my boss would agree to this" or "Your trade could be worth..."—and many other phrases usually remembered by the consumer as an actual "quote"—are nothing more than lead-ins to the salesperson's later excuses as to why he or she cannot make the original deal that was offered. If you reread the phrases above you will see that they all leave the salesperson a way out. They all really implied the word "maybe."

AutoSave Tip

The best two ways to avoid being low-balled are to listen closely to what the salesperson is saying and to attempt to get any offer in writing. This does not mean some handwritten note on the salesperson's business card. It should be a regular sales order with the signature of a manager. Of course, even better than this is following the instructions I have been giving you. If you already know how much the vehicle cost the dealership, the only price you should be negotiating is simply the amount beyond that cost for which the dealership is willing to sell the vehicle.

Trade-in. The phrase "Your trade could be worth as much as..." is the most common. Sure, it could be worth the amount the salesperson tells you if you were to sell it yourself or if it were in perfect condition. Once again, although the salesperson made no promises, this is when most consumers leave the showroom believing they have an offer for their trade-in. In reality, few salespeople are even allowed to appraise a trade-in. This is a job that management usually does. In fact, the salesperson will later get out of the "deal" he or she originally quoted you by telling you that the management won't agree to the amount that was suggested for your trade-in.

Factory orders. Anything that gives the dealership additional time to "work" a customer, such as a factory order, is to its advantage. Some consumers fall prey to the "price increase," while others may have their trades reappraised just prior to delivery. In either case, the more time you have to wait for your vehicle, the more time the dealership has to figure out its game plan. By the time your vehicle arrives you are ready for it. You have already told your friends and family about it and you want it. These are all the necessary ingredients for the dealership to apply pressure. For the dealership, the worst that could happen is a refund of your deposit. You could be out of a vehicle.

Leasing. Sometimes low-balls are indirect. For example, many dealerships and salespeople will quote a lease payment without including sales tax. This can represent $10, $20, $30 a month or more in your payment, and it is certainly easy to justify this increase later on.

Why would a dealership or salesperson low-ball?

The only time salespeople have a shot at selling you is if you are there. Low-balling someone just to get them to come back is a gamble for them, but it is a gamble that often works. Many consumers I've met have told me that if they are low-balled somewhere they will just get up and leave. The industry knows this is not usually the case. A large part of sales is the "wearing down" of consumers. Eventually, they have to say yes to someone. Sure, nobody likes to be lied to, but salespeople know that the customer will be worn down after the frustration of visiting a few dealerships or after waiting weeks for a factory order to come in. If a salesperson can come up with a decent "legitimate" deal and good excuses for why he or she can't keep the original offer, most consumers do end up buying from that salesperson. Often, the consumer's only alternative is continuing to go back and forth between dealerships, or in the case of a factory order, having to start all over again someplace else.

Two of the most common ways to leave yourself open to a low-ball are:

---

1. Telling a salesperson you intend to shop a bunch of dealerships. You almost force him or her into lying to you. That salesperson knows the odds are that someone else will lowball you, so if he or she wants to see you again, it might as well be him or her. You should never disclose your shopping intentions!

2. Shopping price over the phone. Once again, the salesperson has no shot unless he or she can get you into the showroom, and it is a lot easier for the salesperson to lie if you are not face to face. He or she will promise you anything, and then try to sell you everything.

Remember that a good price is easy to get and is the last consideration in getting the "best deal!" If you have chosen the "right" dealership and salesperson, you should never be concerned about being low-balled.

How to deal with your trade-in

Car dealerships love trade-ins. Profits on the sale of used vehicles are almost always higher than on new. You should keep your trade-in and new vehicle price negotiations separate. Dealerships and salespeople like to combine the two so they can deal with one number—the difference. By doing this, you never really know for sure what you are buying the new vehicle for or how much they are actually giving you for your trade-in. Of course, when comparing prices between dealerships, only the bottom-line difference counts.

Two of the most frustrating things for a salesperson are forgetting to ask the customer if he or she has a trade-in and the customer who says he or she doesn't and then pops one in at the last minute. Remember, the salesperson is going to look for every possible reason to offer you less money than your trade is worth. If the person knows up front that you are trading a vehicle, he or she will often offer you a price on the new vehicle you can't refuse and then make up the difference by pointing out every fault on your trade-in. If you have read the beginning of this section and the section on determining the value of your current vehicle, you won't need to fall prey to these games. If you haven't done so already, you should first read "How to determine the value of your current vehicle" on page 42 in Chapter 2.

Closing the deal

Signing a sales order or giving a deposit does not mean that you have a deal. From the dealership's viewpoint, you have only made it an offer. Not until management has countersigned the sales order, and the sales order contains an actual vehicle V.I.N., has the deal actually been made.

AutoSave Tip

When the deal is completed, make sure a manager has countersigned the contract and that you receive a copy.

The salesperson's job is to get you to sign and give a deposit, regardless of whether he or she feels management will accept your offer. The dealership knows that by your signature and deposit you have made some level of mental commitment to the vehicle. What usually happens is that, regardless of the deal you have offered, management will not accept it. Abiding by the old saying "You can't get what you don't ask for," management will often "pencil" your offer in red and send the salesperson back to try to get more money. They know that every minute your signature is on that paper and the deposit is in their hands your mental commitment to the vehicle grows stronger. This is why many dealerships won't even look at your offer unless you sign it and give them money.

At this point the selling process is half over and now it is time to "work" you. There is little that you can actually do about this process other than understand that it takes place and why it works. If you really want to get the dealership riled up, when it comes back looking for more money, offer less than you originally did. This will usually settle everything down. Refer to "Choosing the 'right' dealership" on page 46 in Chapter 2 and "Choosing the 'right' salesperson" on page 66 for information on how to avoid this situation.

The full serial number of the vehicle should always appear on the sales contract. Compare the numbers with the actual vehicle that you have looked at. Many dealerships stock identical vehicles and you may not get the one that you thought you bought or test drove. As a salesman, I was trained to pick the oldest vehicle out of the identical vehicles we had in stock and write up the deal with it, regardless of which one I actually showed the customer. In some cases, it might be a pre-price increase unit that we would make extra money on. In others, it was nothing more than getting rid of older inventory that was subject to the wear and tear of life in the storage lot.

Summary

While I was writing my book, I happened to mention to people that there was a section on making negotiating easy, and the first response I usually got was, "Wow, that must be your longest chapter." At first, this worried me. Maybe people were going to expect a lot more than I was giving them. Fortunately, after many people read my book, their responses were quite different: They were pleased to find out there wasn't much to learn to make negotiating easy. What new rules, then, should you have learned from this section?

1. First of all, becoming an educated consumer is definitely one of the rules. The information that you learn by taking the time to read a book such as this one is going to make negotiating easy.

2. Never shop price! If you know what dealer cost is, or at least ask to see the dealer's invoice, and your offer is a reasonable amount of profit above that cost, you have all but totally eliminated negotiating. If this is the only tip you learn from this book, that's all right, because based on 95 percent of the consumers I have met in the 15-plus years I was in the business, this tip completely turns around the typical consumer's shopping experience!

3. If you have a trade-in, you must have a realistic view of its value to a dealership. Refer to "How to determine the value of your current vehicle" on page 42 in Chapter 2.

4. Never get low-balled! You can only be low-balled if you do not follow the rules I have given you.

"Business manager," "finance manager," "delivery manager"

No matter what name this person goes by, his or her position exists in almost every dealership. For consistency, I will refer to him or her as the "business manager." This job is almost always the same. The person is there to make the other two-thirds profit referred to as the "back-end." After you have finished with the salesperson, he or she is the person you are usually introduced to. He or she handles your financing, after-sell and often the delivery of your vehicle. I have known many business managers who had an income between $80,000 and $120,000 a year or more, mostly from commissions. They are able to make these commissions because few consumers shop with the "big picture" in mind; instead, they concentrate most of their efforts on the "price" of the vehicle. It is the business manager on whom you need to concentrate. Whether you actually get a "good deal" depends on how you deal with him or her.

Your introduction to the business manager is often a deception in itself. After you have made your deal with the car salesperson, the last thing you want to hear is that you are being introduced to someone else who is going to try to sell you financing, rust-proofing, an extended warranty, an alarm or anything else from which he or she and the dealership can make money. So, instead, the business manager is often introduced as someone who has to put your deal in the computer or maybe as the person who will give you the receipt for your deposit. Regardless of the introduction given, you will almost always have to meet and deal with him or her. This person is going to offer you everything and anything to take advantage of the emotions involved with the purchase of a new vehicle. Not to say that you may not want some of these items, but the important thing is your decision to *buy* them rather than have them *sold* to you.

Previously, I stated that a dealership makes back-end profits from how you pay for the vehicle and what you purchase along with it. I also stated that the business manager was responsible for making these profits. What I didn't explain to you is how these profits are often made. As I stated in the very beginning of this book, I am not implying that everyone in the automobile industry practices misleading or deceptive sales techniques, but what I am about to expose to you is one of the most commonly used practices I have seen in every dealership I have worked for.

One of the easiest ways to take advantage of a consumer is with a monthly payment. We take it for granted that if rates are the same, payments will be, too. The business manager counts on this. He or she knows that as long as you are quoted a competitive rate, your payment can be inflated with items that he or she is about to try to sell you. Sometimes you pay for them and don't even know it! Let's take a closer look at how this commonly used technique works.

Imagine that you just made the deal on your new vehicle and you know that you need to finance $10,000 for 48 months. You ask the salesperson what interest rate the dealership is offering. He or she leaves (to go talk to the business manager) and comes back and tells you that the rate is about 10 percent. Ah hah, you think. You're a smart shopper, and you've done your homework. You tell the salesperson that you already called your bank and it said it would give you a loan for 9 percent. The salesperson leaves once again and comes back and states that the business manager is willing to match your bank's rate.

You're feeling pretty good about yourself right now. Your next question is what the monthly payment will be. The salesperson once again leaves, then comes back and tells you that it is $282 per month. Not bad, you think, that's the budget you wanted to be in. Everything seems to be going just fine. Now, let's take a closer look at what actually happened here.

When you called your bank, you asked them only about their rate. You never asked about an exact payment. How could you have? It was not until after you actually made the deal on your vehicle that you knew exactly how much you needed to finance. Because the dealership's rate was the same, you presumed that the payment would be, too. In fact, it really wasn't a presumption on your part, since you probably never gave it a second thought.

What just transpired is that the business manager "packed" your payment. He or she has added something to it other than the amount of the vehicle itself. You can see this by using the amortization tables on pages 176-177. For 48 months, $10,000 should have been a payment of only $253.63, yet you agreed to the $282 the dealer quoted you.

Now the business manager is ready to begin the back-end sales process. You are sitting at his or her desk and you discuss an extended warranty and an alarm system, two items you would like to have on your new vehicle. At this point, you are unaware of the extra $28 per month packed into your payment. You think about the items, which together cost more than $1,000, and ask how much it will add to your monthly payment. The business manager tells you "about $25." As much as you would like these items, you decide that that amount would push you over your budget and you decline. The manager hesitates, maybe leans over the desk, and quietly states that you are a nice person and that you would really like to have these items. "What if I could get them for you and add only $10 a month to your payment?" the manager asks. "Wow," you think. "This is some deal! I don't know how it can be done, but for 10 bucks a month I'm not about to refuse."

As you can see, not only did the manager sell you items that your original payment quote already included, but he or she was able to add an extra $10 a month to the dealership's profit. Even if you had said no to these items, the manager still had the extra $28 a month to play with. He or she simply would have shown the sale and profit of the extras you turned down "internally," that is, only on his own paperwork, and never would have told you about it.

This is why it is so important not only to read and check all the documents that you sign but also to review any of the sales receipts or invoices that you receive after you have picked up your vehicle. The hidden extras can often be found in these documents, because the dealership has and needs a receipt for them for its own records.

As I stated earlier, I have seen this technique used almost every day of my automotive sales career. It works because you don't even know what is being done to you. If you use the amortization tables on pages 176-177 you can avoid this problem. In any case, you should always ask if a payment you are quoted includes any extras. If you ask up front, the salespeople or business manager will almost always expose what they have done. Their excuse will often be that they presumed that these were items you were going to want.

Always get an exact quote. "Around 10 percent" could actually mean 10.75 percent. About $250 a month could actually be $257. What may seem like a trivial amount compared to the thousands of dollars you are spending on the vehicle is often the way the dealership picks up hundreds of dollars in extra profits—by doing nothing more than being vague.

Many banks use a rating system that bases the interest rate you will pay on how strong your credit history is. Because of this, a dealership may not be able to quote you an exact amount at the time you make the deal. Do not sign any finance contract until you know the exact interest rate they intend to charge. Some dealerships that like to "spot" deliver vehicles (meaning that you drive the vehicle home at the time you purchase it), will often have you sign a contract for a rate that is better than they believe you will actually get. A day or two later, they will call you and tell you that the bank rated you differently than they thought it would and that you have to come in and sign a new contract at a higher rate. Sometimes they will even state that if you don't, you have to bring the vehicle back.

Nevertheless, a dealership *can* be the most convenient and competitive place to finance. By using the shopping list on page 182 and amortization tables on pages 176-177, and knowing everything you want before you shop, you have all but eliminated the opportunity to be deceived.

AutoSave Tip

The *ifs*, *arounds* and *abouts* are the most successful part of the automobile sales language. The consumer's failure to ask the "right questions" opens the dealership's window of opportunity.

Summary

Although this was a relatively short section, it was the most important. I've already mentioned that a dealership makes about two-thirds of its profits from the back-end. Hopefully, now you can see why that percentage is so high.

What new rules should you have learned from this section?

1. You should much more concerned with the business manager than the salesperson. How you will pay for your vehicle (whether you pay cash, lease or take out a conventional loan), not what price you get on the vehicle itself, will ultimately determine the overall cost of your purchase.

2. Always get an exact interest quote.

3. If you ask for a monthly payment, always ask for a "clean payment." Tell the salesperson up front that you don't want anything else included in the payment he quotes you.

4. Bring the loan amortization tables with you and check any payment you are quoted.

Taking delivery of your vehicle

When to take delivery of your vehicle

Regardless of how much you learn from this book, purchasing an automobile is still an emotional experience. As I mentioned earlier, the dealership often counts on these emotions to make the sale—not just the sale of the vehicle, but especially the items you purchase along with it. This is a basic example of the psychology of impulse buying.

Because being an educated consumer is not necessarily going to prevent you from making emotional decisions, I strongly suggest that you wait at least 48 to 72 hours after you make your purchase to take delivery of your vehicle. Once away from the dealership, this time will give you the opportunity to reflect on your decisions. This, of course, is something that many car dealerships do not like. Time away from the emotions of the sale often causes what is referred to within the automotive industry as "buyer's remorse." Buyer's remorse is generally when a customer calls the dealership the next day, saying he or she has decided against the rust-proofing, or maybe the alarm, or maybe the vehicle itself. For this reason, a dealership will usually attempt to deliver a vehicle as quickly as possible—one might say, before the ether wears off.

Some dealerships even maintain a policy of "spot" deliveries. They will run a quick credit check on you, have their clean-up crews at hand and let you drive the vehicle home as soon as you have made the decision to purchase it. This process surely eliminates the possibility of buyer's remorse.

AutoSave Tip

Dealerships that practice "spot" deliveries will often use that as a part of their selling technique. In other words, they may make comments such as, "If we agree to sell you the vehicle for that price, do you agree to take delivery of it now?" Don't let this technique be used on you. If they are willing to accept a particular deal, then they are willing to take it tomorrow or the next day, too.

In many states, the law states that the vehicle becomes yours after you have signed all of the paperwork *and* have driven it off the dealership's lot. This is also referred to as "curbing" the vehicle. This law can actually work to your advantage. Regardless of the papers you have signed, you have no obligation to the vehicle until you actually drive it off the lot. In other words, you can cancel the deal any time up until that point.

On the other hand, if you are trying to buy a little thinking time and you inform the dealership that, even though you signed the papers, you want to wait a day or two to pick the vehicle up, the dealership will often find an excuse to have you test drive the vehicle just one more time before you leave. If you do so, you have just made the legal commitment to the vehicle. (Laws vary from state to state. You should check the laws in your state regarding if and how the above situation may affect you.)

What to expect when you're ready to take delivery of your vehicle

Many salespeople equate their commission check with only the actual sale of the vehicle. They will often view the delivery process as time they could better spend trying to make more sales. Because of this, they will often rush you through the process. Don't allow them to! Another reason they may rush you is because they are hiding something. These are some of the things you should expect during delivery:

1. You should be shown how to operate all of the options. The salesperson should also join you for a pre-delivery test drive.

2. You should find out the location and the hours of the service and parts department. Get an explanation of all the service department's policies, including where and when you can leave your vehicle for service. Get the business cards of the department's managers for future reference.

3. You should make sure you fully understand the requirements of your warranty.

4. You should ask what "special service offers" are available to new customers.

5. You should not leave the dealership as a stranger. Ask for a tour and try to meet as many people as possible. Salespeople are often very transient and the more dealership personnel you know, the more people you can turn to with questions or problems if your salesperson is not around.

6. You should inspect every document you sign or are given. Have the salesperson completely explain any areas you are unsure of.

7. You should make sure you have a copy of any document that you sign.

Signing the final paperwork

By the time you are ready to pick up your vehicle, you will most likely feel very trusting and friendly with your salesperson. Remember, the first job of a salesperson is to sell him- or herself. This process usually involves the gaining of your trust. He or she may make you feel like you have made a new friend, but the salesperson is there only for one reason: to make money.

My own personal experience has shown just how this building of trust can make people forget to do the most commonsense things. I would estimate that only 5 percent of the thousands of papers I have had customers sign were actually looked over or read. This is not because they didn't have the common sense to read things before they signed them; it was because I did my job and they trusted me enough to sign wherever I pointed.

A salesperson's language, as previously described, can often be misleading. He or she might put a document in front of you and say, "This is where you sign to activate the warranty on your vehicle." In actuality, you may be signing for an extended warranty that has been packed into your payments. Don't rely on the salesperson's definition of what you are signing. Take the time to read everything you are given and have him or her thoroughly explain anything you are unsure of.

AutoSave Tip

As covered in the section on business managers on page 88, items packed into a deal can be easy to overlook. Remember, the easiest way for the dealership to sell you something is to charge you for it without your knowledge. Checking all of your documents at delivery is a second opportunity to pick up on something. Also, if you haven't done so, and most consumers don't, inspect all of the documents that you received or signed when you took delivery of your last vehicle. You may still have the opportunity to cancel items that might have been included without your knowledge. Items such as extended warranties and life, accident and health insurance can be canceled, and you may be entitled to a prorated refund on the unused term of the policy.

One last thing before you drive away

Always inspect your vehicle before you pay for it. Once you have taken delivery, it is very difficult to claim prior damage. Vehicles are often delivered with physical damage or mechanical problems. If the dealership is aware that your vehicle is damaged, it will often try to get you to pay for the vehicle before the problem is discovered. This reduces the likelihood of your backing out of the deal.

If it is dark, move the vehicle into good lighting. If the weather is bad, ask to have the vehicle brought indoors. Check all of your options and make sure there is plenty of fuel. Last, but not least, always test drive the vehicle before any of the paperwork is signed.

AutoSave Tip

Salespeople will often try to lead you away from a problem. They may rush to open the door for you, acting polite. This may be because there is something they are trying to hide. The same can hold true for a "quick" showing of how the options work. Don't let the salesperson operate them. You should operate them yourself and take as much time as you feel you need!

Summary

As I am sure you are learning, there is a lot more to the purchase of a vehicle than just negotiating a deal. A dealership's selling process doesn't end until you have driven the vehicle off the lot. When it comes to taking delivery of your vehicle, what new rules should you have learned?

1. You have just made a major investment. Do not rush through the delivery process or allow the salesperson to do so.

2. Thoroughly check out the vehicle before you sign any papers!

3. Ask questions and read as much of the paperwork as possible before you sign anything. (You do not have to take this to extremes. For example, an automobile manufacturer's finance contract will be pretty legitimate. There is really no need for you to read all of it. You should, though, be checking all the numbers that have been filled in.)

4. Whenever possible, give yourself at least 48 to 72 hours after you have made the deal before you schedule the actual delivery of the vehicle.

Chapter 4

Payment: making the choice

Your options

Once you have established your budget, the next step is deciding how those numbers are going to apply. Not enough people consider the option of leasing, explained in Chapter 5, because they are unfamiliar with how it works. Few people consider paying cash because it isn't within their budget. Most people jump headfirst into financing without first learning about its variations and possible alternatives.

With any depreciating product, you should always consider your options. Automobile manufacturers have been offering some very exciting incentive programs the last few years to help sell their vehicles, which I am sure will continue for years to come.

The way you choose to pay for your vehicle can have the largest effect on your overall cost of ownership. Regardless of which method you have been considering, I suggest you look at all of the alternatives.

Paying cash?

Many economists claim that the best way to deal with a losing proposition, such as the purchase of an automobile, is by paying cash. Not only is this not an option available for most consumers, it is not always the best choice.

Many consumers are under some misguided and antiquated impression that by letting the dealership know that they intend to pay cash, they are going to be able to make a better deal. I suppose there may still be some small businesses that consider cash payments to be a way of beating the tax system, but telling the salespeople that you intend to pay cash can possibly hurt you.

Dealerships make money from financing! Telling the salespeople you are going to pay cash is telling them they are going to make less money! If they are not going to make additional profits from financing the vehicle for you, they may not be as flexible with how much of a discount they are willing to give you on the selling price of the vehicle itself. Even if you have firmly committed yourself to paying cash, tell the salesperson that you're not sure how you intend to pay for the vehicle until the deal is finalized.

If you are considering paying cash for your vehicle, make sure you weigh it against the alternatives. If a manufacturer is offering a very low finance or lease rate, it may pay to keep your money in the bank. The more you put down on a vehicle, the more you stand to lose.

There is a very creative way of financing that I consider an excellent alternative to paying cash in many cases. In recent years, a new form of lease, generically known as "the prepaid lease," was created. In essence, an automobile manufacturer will guarantee a vehicle's minimum future value two years after your purchase date and then subtract that value from the purchase price of the vehicle now. For example, let's say you are looking at a $20,000 vehicle, and the manufacturer says that vehicle will be worth at least $12,000 two years from now. You pay only $8,000 today and then have the option in two years of paying the other $12,000 to own the vehicle. Simply stated, the concept is not having to pay for the whole vehicle at once but also not having a monthly payment. (This was a very basic explanation of how this program works. It is explained in more detail in Chapter 5).

Where should you go for financing?

There are generally three sources that consumers turn to when they have decided to finance a vehicle. The following are some of the pros and cons of those choices.

Dealerships. The car dealership can often be your best and easiest place to finance. Like a shopping mall, it offers one-stop shopping. Because you are already there buying your vehicle, what could be more convenient? Car dealerships are also the only place where you can take advantage of incentive programs offered by the automobile manufacturer, such as special interest rates. In most cases, the dealerships have a few finance sources. This allows them to shop rates just as you would. Another advantage dealerships have is their relationship with the banks. Their volume of business makes them valuable customers. Unlike your private bank, which may require two to seven working days to give you an answer on your loan application, a dealership will often have an answer in just a few hours. Financing is a high profit area for dealerships, but as long as they are giving you a competitive rate and payment, this shouldn't bother you. As explained earlier, the toughest part is getting around the selling practices of the "business manager."

Some dealerships offer what is known as "in-house" financing. This means that they are loaning out their own money. Be very careful about their terms. Some dealerships offering this type of financing have been known to repossess vehicles right after the very first late payment, and you could stand to lose everything you have paid for the vehicle up until that time.

AutoSave Tip

If you have had some credit problems, the car dealership may be your answer. Because a salesperson is anxious to sell a vehicle, he or she will make an extra effort to help you with your loan. Dealerships operate under two basic programs with the banks: "recourse" and "nonrecourse." A recourse dealership is responsible to the bank for your loan. The dealerships that take this level of responsibility will often get loans approved that banks had turned down on their own. Of course, the problem is that the more of a gamble a loan is considered to be, the higher an interest rate the dealership is going to charge. Only you can decide what value you place on the opportunity to improve your credit rating. With non-recourse dealers, the banks have the final say, but because of their volume of business, nonrecourse dealerships can still help influence the results of loan applications.

Your personal bank. If you are a good customer of your bank, you may be offered special interest rates. A bank can often provide services the dealerships can't, such as automatic payment withdrawal from one of your accounts. However, you do have the hassle of going back and forth to apply for and get your funds. The bank may also keep you waiting many days for its answer.

Credit unions. Some credit unions offer highly competitive interest rates for their members, as well as the ability to take the loan payments out of their paychecks. Credit unions' terms should be looked at closely. Some state that if you leave your job, the balance of your loan becomes due in full. Make sure that you ask about any and all conditions. Like banks, credit unions will often take a long time to give you an answer and create the hassle of going back and forth to get your funds.

AutoSave Tip

Almost every time you apply for any type of a loan, a report is sent to a consumer credit reporting agency. Even if you do not accept a loan, an "inquiry" remains on your credit report. Avoid submitting a lot of loan applications. Accumulated inquiries begin to look "questionable" to those rating your future loan applications.

Summary

Today, there are many ways of creative financing that may be better and cheaper alternatives to paying cash, and if you do intend to finance, there are a lot of positive reasons to do so with the car dealership. As with everything else discussed in this book, you must be aware of games that can be played against you. What new rules should you have learned from this section?

1. Cash is not always the best bet. I have always been a firm believer that before I say no to something, I would at least like to know something about what I am saying no to. This should be your attitude when exploring the alternatives to paying cash.

2. Financing through a car dealership can often be the cheapest and most convenient way to go. Just be sure to always keep both eyes open.

3. Be careful with your credit report. You should not let anyone run a credit check on you unless you have committed to purchasing a particular vehicle at a particular dealership.

"Special finance" departments

Many dealerships are turning to "special finance" departments to increase their profits. These departments are specifically designed for, and often prey on, consumers with weak or poor credit ratings. You've seen the ads. "Been turned down before, we'll get you financed," "Poor Credit, No Credit, No Problem," "Bankruptcies, Not a Problem" and many others. There is an old adage that basically states that there is

---

no such thing as something for nothing. That adage certainly holds true here. The banks and car dealerships that offer these services are not rich philanthropists dedicated to giving money away. They are smart businesspeople looking at any angle they can to make more from a consumer, often more than they should really be entitled to. I am not saying that "special finance" departments have no place in the car business, or that you should not necessarily make use of one. You must simply be aware of just how much it is going to cost you to possibly build or reestablish your credit rating. Although you don't want to fill your credit report up with inquiries from numerous banks, you should not simply take the answer from one bank or, for that matter, one dealer. I have met many consumers whose credit was not as bad as they thought it was. Situations where the bank was willing to grant a *reasonable* interest rate but the dealership or salesperson still convinced the consumer that he or she had to pay a much higher rate in order to get the loan. Realize that part of "back-end" profits that we have touched on include the fact that for each percentage rate that the dealership charges you over what the bank is charging it is realized as profit to the dealership. Keep this in mind anytime you are considering a loan that has an above-average interest rate. Don't make the assumption yourself that because of your credit rating, you deserve to pay a ridiculously high interest rate. Do some homework and even discuss the issue with the bank that you normally do business with. Even if the bank won't give you the loan, it may be able to help advise you on what type of rate you may end up having to pay to get a loan elsewhere.

AutoSave Tip

Leasing can often be an excellent alternative to paying high interest rates. Unlike years ago, some banks are more flexible with lease credit applications than they are with conventional finance applications. To date, I am unaware of any interest or lease rate variations based on the credit strength of the applicant, unlike with conventional loans. In other words, it is usually a simple yes or no approval. This means that if you are approved, you will pay the same rate that even someone with a solid credit rating will pay.

Be sure that you fully understand all of the terms and conditions that are a part of any special finance contract. Often these terms or conditions can easily lead to defaulting on the loan or to paying an unusual amount of interest, late fees or surcharges. As always, buyers (borrower) beware!

Computing your overall cost

How financing alternatives can affect your overall cost

When we get accustomed to something, we accept that this is the only way that it can be. Most consumers look at financing this way. If they can't afford a three-year loan or lease, they feel that their only alternative is to go to a four-year. If they can't afford a four-year, they go to a five-year or even longer. What happened to the in-between?

Every month that you have a loan you are paying interest that is adding to your overall cost of ownership. Every bank I have ever dealt with was willing to issue loans and leases with flexible terms. Let's look at an example of what this can mean for you financially.

Example: You want to finance $12,000. Your budget shows that you are comfortable with payments of $275 per month. For the example, we will be using an interest rate of 10 percent. First you look into what a four-year loan would do for you.

4 years @ 10% = $304.35 a month x 48 months = a total cost of $14,608.80. *Payment is too high.*

5 years @ 10% = $254.96 a month x 60 months = a total cost of $15,297.60. *Payment is low, but at what extra cost?*

What happened to the in-between? How about 54 months (4½ years)?

4½ years @ 10% = $276.86 a month x 54 months = a total cost of $14,950.44.

Not only is the payment right where you wanted your budget to be, but you have saved $347.16 in total interest charges by doing nothing more than cutting six months from your loan.

Let's take a look at a couple of other examples of creative financing that can affect your overall cost in ways that you may not have considered.

Delayed payment programs. Some finance programs can delay the due date of your first payment by as much as six months. More likely than not you have already heard numerous advertisements for this kind of offer regarding other items, such as furniture and appliances. Not having to make payments for a while can seem like a very enticing situation, but at what cost to you? Realize that although the beginning of your payment cycle may be deferred, the interest that you pay starts from the first day that you purchased the product. In other words, the interest for the time period that you waited to make your first payment will be spread out over the term of your loan.

AutoSave Tip

Many consumers are using home equity loans to pay for their vehicles. The rates are often very competitive, and you can usually write off the interest on your income taxes. Just be very aware of what you are getting into. You may be putting up your home as collateral for your vehicle.

Deferring a portion of a loan to the end. With leases and balloon loans, you are offered a way of lowering your monthly payments by deferring a portion of your loan to the end. What you may not realize is that doing this still requires you to pay interest on the full selling price of the vehicle. This means that if you want to finance your lease-end purchase option or balloon note payment, you will be paying interest twice on that money—once for the term of the lease or the balloon note, and again on the portion of the vehicle you are actually refinancing.

Although the size of monthly payments is often more important to most consumers than their overall cost, you should always take a look at just what that overall cost is, and once again, remember to consider your alternatives.

AutoSave Tip

How you finance—and for how long—can make a difference of thousands of dollars in your overall cost of ownership. Remember to compare the total cost of your decision
with the total cost of the available alternatives.

L, A & H (life, accident and health insurance)

Whether you are taking out an auto loan or any other kind of
loan, most lending institutions offer loan insurance. The purpose of
the life policy is to pay off the balance of the loan should the borrower
pass away. The accident and health policy is there to cover your loan
payments in the event that you become injured or ill. Most policies
state that you must be out of work for at least seven consecutive days.
At this point, with a doctor's verification, your monthly payment(s)
will be made by the insurance company for the length of time you are
out of work due to your illness or injury. Most policies are retroactive
to the first day of work that you missed, even though you had to wait
a week to quality for the benefits.

Because selling insurance on loans is another profit area for the
dealership, be cautious. I have heard consumers told that the bank
required the insurance as part of their loan approval. This is *never* the
case. Life and/or accident and health insurance is strictly a personal
option. Here are some other things you should know about this option:

Who can be covered? Although it can vary, the age limit for
most policies is 65. If more than one person is on the loan, one or both
individuals can be covered.

**Do you have to buy the life policy and the accident and
health insurance policy together?** It has been my experience that
the insurance companies will offer the life insurance by itself but not
the accident and health insurance without the life insurance.

Do you have to pay back the insurance company? No, you
pay a monthly premium that is included in your loan payment.

How much will it cost? The size and term of the loan determines the cost. Premiums will also vary among insurance companies. A 48-month $10,000 loan with L, A and H on one borrower will have a premium of about $15 per month, which would multiply out to a total cost (with interest) of $720 for the policies.

The example of premium cost given above is based on purchasing the policy through the lending institution. If you have decided that L, A and H insurance is important to you, you should contact your own private insurance representative. Typically, the premiums that your insurance agent will charge are at least 50 percent less than the premiums charged by the lending institutions.

Almost everyone complains about paying insurance premiums of any kind. The possible financial repercussions of being without insurance certainly make it a consideration to look into. As always, the key is your decision to buy it—not have it sold to you, or worse yet, pay for it without knowing that you have it.

How bank "rating systems" affect the interest rate you will pay

Many banks no longer just decide whether to approve your loan. They have started to use a "rating system." The bank determines your creditworthiness and then assigns a rating to your loan application. It then determines the interest rate it will charge you, based on this rating. Those with an excellent credit rating will be offered the lowest available interest rates, while those with questionable or poor credit may have to pay a steep price for their loan approval. If you don't agree with your rating, question how the bank made its decision.

If you want to question the rating your dealership gave you, call the bank the dealership used and ask to speak with its consumer-lending department. Ask what rating you received and why. This personal contact may expose problems with your credit that you were unaware of, or it may expose an attempt by the dealership to make more profit from your loan by charging you a higher interest rate than the one for which the bank actually rated you. At times, this personal contact may also cause a bank to reconsider its original rating decision in your favor.

When an automobile manufacturer is offering a special interest rate, approval of your loan application will be only a yes or no determination and rating systems usually will not apply. However, if the manufacturer's lending institution is offering money at a very low interest rate, it may be a little more strict about who it decides to approve.

Summary

By not exploring your alternatives, it is easy to make costly mistakes when financing your new vehicle.

Many people are firm believers that you can never have too much insurance. Life, accident and health insurance can be a valuable asset to your auto loan, as long as you are not paying too much for it and it was not forced on you or "packed" into your payments. As with any kind of insurance, when you need it, you are thankful it was there, and if you don't use it, you complain that you paid for it. Only you can decide whether you want it.

While bank-rating systems offer consumers with excellent credit the opportunity to pay lower-than-normal rates and those with weak credit the opportunity to finance their purchases, they also, unfortunately, have opened up another opportunity for deception among car dealerships.

What new rules should you have learned from these sections?

1. Most banks will be flexible about the term of your loan.

2. You have the option, with most auto loans, to protect both your investment and the ability to pay for it with L, A and H insurance.

3. If there is any question in your mind about how your credit has been rated, don't accept the response of the dealership as your only answer. Contact the financial institution directly.

4. Be aware of the many pitfalls associated with "special finance" departments.

Chapter 5

To lease or not to lease?

What is leasing all about, and is it for you?

It's nearly impossible to turn on a TV set or radio, open a newspaper or enter a car dealership and not see or hear the word "lease." The automotive buzzword of the 90s has many consumers confused and often frustrated. Could at least some of the confusion be based on the fact that lease advertising is full of terms, conditions and disclaimers that sound like a foreign language to most of us? Could at least some of the frustration be because almost every other person that you ask has a different opinion about leasing? Why, if leasing is so misunderstood, is the automobile industry pushing it so hard?

Let's first understand why automobile manufactures are pushing the leasing concept. Automobile manufacturers needed a way to get consumers to keep their new vehicles for a shorter period of time. Only a generation or so ago, most consumers traded their vehicles every one to three years. Today, the average age of vehicles on our highways is 5 to 7 years old. With the average lease being only two to three years long, leasing certainly presented itself as a means to increase new car sales.

Another reason leasing has become a feasible financing alternative is the outrageous sticker prices of today's vehicles. With vehicles costing even more than most homes did some time ago, car payments, financed conventionally, are beginning to look more like mortgage payments. At first, the automobile industry simply started to offer longer term car loans. (About 30 years ago, few lending institutions offered loan terms beyond 24 months. Today, there are auto loans up to seven years long!) Offering longer term loans certainly made payments much easier to handle, but it also made consumers keep their vehicles even longer. Increased loan terms created many other problems. Vehicles depreciate much more quickly than they are paid off. Unless consumers made a sizable down payment, they were stuck with the vehicle until the loan was completely paid off. Keeping a vehicle for an extended period of time meant more maintenance and repair bills, which naturally lead to bad feelings about the vehicle itself. This lead to a problem with owner loyalty. With all of the new models, and even brand names, offered to consumers almost every year, the idea that the grass was greener on the other side worked its way into automotive shopping habits.

By offering consumers a financial means to keep their vehicles for a shorter period of time—a period that represents the least amount of maintenance and the most reliability—leasing greatly increases customer satisfaction, thus increasing the potential for greater brand loyalty.

Another benefit that leasing has for the automobile industry is control. Most leased vehicles have to be returned to the dealership, or at least the same brand dealership, from which they were leased. The automobile industry spends billions of dollars a year to get consumers into their showrooms. With a lease, they show up because they have to.

As I'm sure you can see, leasing is and will continue to be an asset to automobile sales. But is that all there is to it? Has the automobile industry, by helping themselves, actually also helped you? Is there really such a thing as a win-win situation here? Before I answer that question, I think it is important that you understand a little bit more of what leasing is all about.

Why people do or don't consider leasing

First, let's look at why some consumers *don't* consider leasing.

They know little or nothing about it. If this is your case, don't feel bad. Many of the car salespeople I have worked with also know little or nothing about it, and they are the ones who are supposed to be educating the consumer.

They believe leasing means they don't own the vehicle. When you finance, you don't own the vehicle either, the lender does. You only own the vehicle after the loan is paid in full. With leasing, your payments pay for only part of the vehicle for the time that you use it. Most leases give you what is known as a "lease-end purchase option," the opportunity to own the vehicle by paying the balance.

Note: *It has always amazed me why consumers want to own their automobiles! This is a product that depreciates in value and costs you more money the longer you keep it. Would you tell a stockbroker that you had $20,000 to invest, and that his or her job was to turn it into*

$10,000 in a 3- or 4-year period? I know, maybe I'm not being fair here. Cars are a necessity and investments are a luxury, but that still does not change the basic math. The bottom line is that cars, all of them, are a losing proposition. To me, the only way to win is to learn how to cut your loses, and in my view, not paying for the entire vehicle to start with is certainly one way to help accomplish this.

They believe that leasing costs more. In almost every case I have known, the only time a lease costs more than buying is when the consumer made or was sold a bad lease deal. There are times when special finance programs can outweigh the benefits of leasing, but on the whole, the basic cost of a lease should either be a little less, the same as or just a little more than conventional financing. Let me explain that a little further. Right off the bat, consumers feel that if they lease a vehicle and then don't exercise their purchase option, all they have done is thrown away the payments that they made for the past few years. Once again, we are back to the feeling that when we lease we don't own. Think about it this way: Even if you had paid cash for the vehicle and then decided to sell it a few years down the road, are you going to get all of your money back? Of course not! You will always pay for the depreciation of the product you are driving regardless of how you choose to pay for it. Basically, that's all lease payments are—simply paying for the depreciation of the product. (Other benefits of leasing are discussed further on.)

Leasing doesn't offer consumers any tax benefits. Today's tax laws don't allow you to write off a loan, either. Except for businesses, leasing is not a matter of write-offs but of taking advantage of alternate means of financing that can save you money. If you are in a situation that you can write off a lease payment, I always like to call that the icing on the cake, but it is not the cake itself.

They once had problems with leasing or know someone who did. Once again, the reliability and reputation of whom you do business with are going to be the keys to your satisfaction. I have never known leasing itself to be a problem, but I have known of many individual leases that were. This was because of the deal that was made, not because of leasing itself. It should also be noted that leasing has gone through tremendous changes in recent years. The basic structure of most leases today eliminates the majority of problems that consumers had with leases of the past.

They believe they're stuck with the vehicle for the whole lease term. Like a conventional loan, a lease can be paid off early; you are simply obligated to fulfill the full dollar amount of the contract, not the term. You can trade in a leased vehicle, sell it or buy it outright. Early buyout and trading in a lease are discussed further on.

Those were just a few of the primary examples of why some consumers often overlook the option of leasing. Now let's look at the reasons some consumers *do* consider it.

Why people do consider leasing

Availability. Leasing is no longer just for the executive or business owner. Many lending and consumer protection laws have changed to help make leasing a consideration for almost anyone. In fact, the majority of leasing programs and incentives offered by the automobile industry today are designed for and aimed at the average consumer.

Shorter terms and lower payments. A survey of financial institutions has shown that most consumers who take out a 60-month conventional loan call up the bank asking for their payoff amount at the 37th month. This is because, even though it took a 60-month loan to get their payments where they wanted them to be, most consumers don't want to keep a vehicle for five years. Because you are not paying for the entire vehicle when you have a lease, you can usually shorten the loan term to 24 or 36 months and still have a payment that is about the same as a 60-month conventional loan or lower than a normal 48-month loan.

Trade-in. When you buy a vehicle and pay for the whole thing, you must either trade it or sell it to get rid of it. With a lease, you don't pay for the whole vehicle and you can walk away from it at the end. You have paid only the depreciation for the time that you used it. Of course, an additional benefit is not having to spend money on advertising your vehicle, which includes the prospect of giving out your telephone number and having strangers call and come to your home. I have yet to meet a consumer who enjoys the prospect of trading-in or selling their vehicle. This process is totally eliminated with leasing.

Maintenance. Having a new vehicle every two or three years all but eliminates your chances of ever having major, often unexpected, repair bills, and most maintenance costs will be limited to nothing more than gas and oil changes.

Depreciation. Consumers are recognizing the most basic of financial principles: Invest as much as possible into something that appreciates and as little as possible into something that depreciates, such as a car. Put $5,000 down towards the purchase of an automobile and in three years it has depreciated to about $3,000. Lease, and put the same $5,000 in the bank, and in three years it has appreciated to about $6,000 (based on 6 percent interest compounded yearly). In other words, leasing simply offers you a way to be more creative with what you do with your hard-earned money.

Incentives. More of the lease rebates and incentive programs offered by the manufacturers are better than the incentive programs that they are offering for conventional financing.

Less risk. This is probably one of the most important reasons to lease. Any lease with a written purchase option puts the lender at risk for the future value of the vehicle. If you walk away from it at the end, the lender owns it regardless of its current market value. A good example is a new model vehicle that friends of mine had leased. It never became popular, so its production was discontinued. Although $8,000 had been deferred to the lease-end purchase option, the vehicle's market value at lease-end had dropped to only $2,000. My friends simply walked away, while the lessor had to suffer the $6,000 loss. This situation could have worked out the other way. If the car was more valuable than its lease-end purchase option, they could have bought it, sold it or possibly traded it in for a profit. Basically, when you lease, you are making the bank play fortune-teller. It has to guess what the vehicle might be worth at the end of your lease term. This amount is actually the amount of the vehicle that you are not paying for. I know that I certainly prefer someone else taking the risk of what my vehicle might be worth a few years down the road.

Write-offs. Anyone who uses a car or truck for business, full- or part-time, will usually discover excellent tax benefits.

Consistency. Many consumers look forward to their last car payment only to discover the unknown factor of repair bills. Those who are aware that they will always have some kind of monthly vehicle expense like the consistency and dependability a lease can offer.

AutoSave Tip

Even if you intend to keep your vehicle longer than most lease terms, leasing can still be a good option. A lease with a purchase option can have a two-fold benefit. A business can usually write off the entire monthly payment, including interest, but usually not taxes, for the entire lease term. Once the business exercises the purchase option, it receives the current business depreciation—offered under current I.R.S. tax laws—of 20 percent per year for five years on the purchase option price. A three-year lease, plus the buyout, can give the business eight years of write-off.

Having a choice. Many consumers like the idea of not having to commit to the full purchase price of a vehicle the day they decide to buy it, like they would had they signed a conventional loan contract. With a lease, you have deferred a good portion of the cost of the vehicle to a purchase option, something that you don't have to decide on until the lease is up. It's like taking an extended test drive while only paying for the depreciation on the vehicle.

Now that we have looked at some of the main reasons why people do or don't consider leasing and why leasing has become so important to automobile manufacturers, let's take a look at why car dealerships and car salespeople have so eagerly agreed to jump on the leasing bandwagon.

The priority for a dealership, like for a manufacturer, is to increase sales. Selling vehicles to customers who are going to keep them for a shorter period of time will certainly accomplish this. The motivations of some dealerships, however, go a step further. Unfortunately, lease lending laws still offer those dealerships that choose to practice misleading or deceptive sales techniques many windows of profit opportunity. Many lease contracts still don't require a selling price to be disclosed. This means that regardless of the selling price you negotiate with the dealership, your lease can be based on any selling price the dealership can get away with. Once again, I find it necessary to repeat that the reliability and reputation of who you do business with will be the keys to your overall satisfaction.

Lease Disclosure

Although full disclosure has yet to be made into federal law, many financial institutions have started to make "selling price," also referred to as "capitalized cost," disclosure a standard part of their lease contracts. I would advise that you deal only with a lease contract that offers this type of disclosure. Anything else is leaving yourself open to problems.

What types of leases are there?

Although each state has its own lending laws, today, there is only one kind of lease that is available to consumers, and it is referred to as a closed-end lease. The only difference between most closed-end leases is whether they contain a "purchase-option," and who has first right to that option if it is offered. Not too long ago there were also leases that were referred to as "open-end." Today, open-end leases are available only in some areas and for commercial use only. Basically an open-end lease places the burden of responsibility for what the future value of the vehicle is on the lessee, not the lessor. In other words, if the financial institution guesses wrong on what the residual value of a vehicle is (the amount you are not paying for when you lease), the lessee can be held responsible for any difference between how much of the vehicle they hadn't paid for and how much its current market value is. This got a lot of consumers in trouble years ago and I am very glad to see that it is no longer a part of consumer leasing options.

Closed-end further explained. As was discussed earlier, a closed-end lease is basically were the financial institution is forced to guess what the vehicle being leased is going to be worth at the end of the lease. This then becomes the amount of the vehicle that you don't pay for. What you end up with, with this type of lease, are options. The first option is to simply walk away from the vehicle when the lease term is completed, having responsibility only for any excess wear and tear. If the lender made a mistake with the vehicle's projected lease-end value, once again, the amount of the vehicle that you have not paid for, the lender takes the loss, not you. In some cases, the vehicle may be worth more than the lender had anticipated. In this case, if your lease gives you the "first" option to purchase, you may wish to purchase the vehicle, or possibly have the opportunity to trade it in or sell it for a profit. Basically, what you are doing when you lease, is simply paying for only a portion of the vehicle over a pre-determined period of time and then being given the ability to make your final decision as to the balance at the end of the purchase agreement, instead of at the beginning. Leasing offers you the best form of protection against an automobile's market value fluctuations.

What restrictions or penalties can you expect with a lease?

None! I say this only because the words "restrictions" and "penalties" imply that you must pay something extra for nothing. These terms make consumers misunderstand or fear leasing. Let's take a look at how and why these terms don't really apply and get a better look at just how leasing really works.

Mileage. Most leases use 12,000 to 15,000 miles per year as a *guideline* and state that there is a cost per mile "fee" if you exceed it. Let's say that you leased a vehicle for three years but ended up driving it 60,000 miles. Now the lease has ended and you want to turn the vehicle back in, but the dealership charges you $2,250 for the excess mileage. (This amount is based on 15 cents for each mile of the extra 15,000 miles you drove. Per-mile costs will vary. There is no mileage charge if you choose to purchase the vehicle.) This sounds like a penalty, doesn't it? Think of it this way: Let's say you went out and bought two identical vehicles for cash. In three years, you drove one 45,000 miles and the other 60,000 miles. Now you decide to trade or sell them both. Isn't the vehicle with 60,000 miles going to be worth a lot less money? Even though you paid cash for it, a smaller return on your investment makes that vehicle cost you more than the other one. So, excess mileage fees are not a "penalty" but simply the price you pay for over-using the vehicle.

A lease has to have guidelines because, unlike cash or conventional financing, you don't pay for the whole vehicle and you have the option of simply giving it back. If you know that you are going to drive 20,000 miles a year, this can be written into the lease from the start. Your payments will be increased to compensate for the fact that you are depreciating a vehicle more quickly than normal, but on the other hand, your lease-end purchase option will usually be decreased by the extra amount you are paying up front. Using the example at the beginning of this section, the $2,250 would be spread over your 36 lease payments, and that same $2,250 would be deducted from the lease-end purchase option.

Not all lease contracts lower your purchase option. In other words, even if you claim the excess mileage and pay for it up front, the price for which you can purchase the vehicle at lease end will not change.

AutoSave Tip

Many consumers feel that they cannot lease because they drive too many miles per year. The fact is, the more you drive the better leasing can be. In almost every case, it will cost you less to pay for a high-mileage lease than it will cost you to purchase the vehicle and then dispose of (trade-in or resell) the vehicle. Yes, your payments will go up, but when compared to how much you would lose if you paid cash or conventionally financed the vehicle, leasing will almost always make you a winner.

Insurance. Many consumers are under the impression that their insurance rates will go up because they lease. Although my primary experience is in the New York metropolitan area—which, by the way, has some of the highest insurance rates in the nation—I have never seen an insurance company charge more simply because a vehicle is leased. As with a conventional loan, you do have to carry full coverage insurance, and there may be limitations to the size of your deductibles.

AutoSave Tip

There is an insurance option called "GAP" specifically designed for leases. Some consumers run into financial problems if their vehicle is stolen or totaled early on in the lease. They often owe more than the vehicle is worth. A GAP policy, which costs around $100 a year, covers the difference between what you owe to the bank and what your insurance company pays you. *Most* lending institutions offer this coverage for free with leases. Be sure to check with your dealership whether your lease automatically comes with it. If it doesn't, I strongly recommend you get it.

Normal depreciation. This clause, which is in every lease contract, usually causes consumers much concern. As with mileage, if you over-depreciate a vehicle, it is going to cost you something. This clause is there to protect the company that is guaranteeing your vehicle's lease-end value. These companies do not expect your vehicle to come back in showroom condition, but they do expect a "reasonable" amount of wear and tear. If you're a careless smoker and there are burn holes in the fabric, expect to be charged for them. If you put 50,000 miles on a vehicle and never replaced the tires, expect to be charged for them. These are some of the things that can cause a vehicle to be worth less money, *no matter how you paid for it.*

The problem with the lease clause "normal depreciation" is how vague it is. Basically, you are at the mercy of whomever inspects your vehicle at lease end. This is why I keep repeating that "the reliability and reputation of whom you do business with..." are so important. In this case, it can determine the overall cost of your lease. An experience I had while working for an independent lease company can best illustrate how this works.

We had numerous financial sources to handle our lease contracts. They all offered us money within half of a percentage point of each other. We did, however, have one other financial source that kept attempting to get our business by offering us 2 percent less than our other sources. Because many of the vehicles we specialized in were $35,000 and more (in 1986), this 2 percent difference would have had a very noticeable effect on the monthly payments we could offer. Because most consumers go out and shop "price"—or in the case of a lease, "monthly payments"—we could very easily have increased our short-term business by using this financial source. Fortunately, the lease company I worked for was more interested in long-term customer satisfaction. You see, we knew that although this financial source offered money for 2 percent less, it was also known to inspect vehicles meticulously at lease-end. Its definition of normal depreciation would more than make up for the profit it lost by lending money at a lower interest rate. The lending institutions and lease companies that use the clause "normal depreciation" as a profit-making gimmick have given many consumers a bad experience with leasing. Again, keeping the "big picture" in mind, what seems to be the "best price" is not always the "best deal!" (See the following, "From whom should you lease?")

Obligation to term. A lease can be terminated at any time. As with any loan, however, you are obligated to complete your financial transaction. You must take caution to fully understand the terms you are being offered. Some lease contracts impose heavy fees for early lease termination. The fees generally make up the difference between how much the vehicle has actually depreciated and the amount you have paid so far for its use. (Read "From whom should you lease?" and "Terminating early or buying out a lease" on page 130 to learn more about handling these situations.)

What you've read so far should have continued to show you that leasing is nothing more than a creative way of financing. It does not have to cost you more than any other type of purchase and, in fact, can often cost you less. Consumers, however, seem to associate the terms "restriction" and "penalty" with leases because these terms often relate to the future value of the vehicle and possible fees for wear and tear. Remember, regardless of how you pay for your vehicle (including cash), excess wear and tear will always end up costing you money in the long run.

From whom should you lease?

Basically, you have two choices: the car dealership and the independent lease company. Sometimes they are a little hard to distinguish, because many car dealerships have established their own independent lease companies.

Not to say independent lease companies have nothing to offer, but based on my definition of the "best deal," you will almost always get the best deal from the car dealership. Let's take a look at some of the pros and cons of both.

Price. It is rare that independent lease companies get a better price on a vehicle than the consumer. They have to shop at the same car dealerships you do. Although some of them can get what are known as "fleet rebates," these are generally in lieu of individual consumer rebates. Fleet rebates will rarely offer a purchase price advantage. The fact that a lease company may buy in volume will also offer little or no price advantage. Dealer invoice is the same regardless of who the buyer is. A consumer can usually purchase a vehicle for the same price that the independent lease company can.

Monthly payments. Because the purchase price (cap cost) of the vehicle is basically the same whether you or the lease company buys it from the dealership, a variance in monthly payments will be caused by other factors, such as the percentage of the vehicle deferred to the end of the lease, which is the vehicle's residual value, or the money factor (similar to interest), you are being charged to borrow the money. To understand the concept of the percentage of the vehicle that is being deferred to the residual value, think of a lease as a see-saw. The more you defer to one end, the less of the vehicle you are paying for on the other and the lighter the monthly payments. The amount, or percentage, of the vehicle that is to be deferred is entirely up to the individual finance source. It is up to this source to determine (gamble) how much of the vehicle's value it might be stuck with if you choose to walk away from the car at lease-end.

Lease rates. Lease rates can vary quite a bit. Because lease companies usually get their money from conventional sources, such as local banks, rarely can they compete with rates that are often subsidized by the automobile manufacturer's lending institutions. Finance companies such as Ford Motor Credit, General Motors Acceptance Corporation, Chrysler Credit and others will often offer money at a loss to help sell more vehicles.

AutoSave Tip

Lease rates and interest rates are not the same thing. Lease rates can have other fees built into them and should not be considered APRs (actual percentage rates) unless specified as such. If you were to amortize a lease rate into an interest rate, it will often turn out to be a much higher figure. Don't be fooled by a number. Be sure to total your payments and lease-end purchase option so you can take a better look at what is being offered to you. (An example is shown further on).

Residual values. This is where independent lease companies often have an advantage. Fighting to compete with the manufacturers, independent finance sources are often willing to take a greater gamble with the projected lease-end value of a vehicle. But although they may defer a greater percentage of your vehicle to the residual value, thus lowering your monthly payment, this may offer you only a monthly payment advantage, and not an overall cost advantage. Remember, if you have to or choose to purchase your vehicle at lease-end, you may have to pay a lot more for it than it is worth.

AutoSave Tip

Although most consumers who lease do not concern themselves with a vehicle's lease-end purchase price, statistically, a majority of consumers do look to purchase their vehicles at lease end. None of us can foresee the circumstances of our future. Remember to keep the "big picture" in mind and always look at the total possible costs of any deal you get yourself involved with.

Normal depreciation. With an independent lease company, you often don't know who is financing your lease contract. In fact, many financial sources often sell their "paper" (your contract) to other companies. The company that you finance your lease with and the one that you turn your vehicle over to at lease-end may not be the same. You will have little or no idea who will be appraising the normal depreciation of your vehicle. Because automobile manufacturers' finance institutions are tied into the business of selling vehicles, they are often more considerate with this contract clause. If the lease company, and not the bank, is responsible for your vehicle at lease-end, its view of normal depreciation may be tied into how well business is doing. If things are slow, the lease company and/or financial institution may be looking for the "clause" they need to help raise extra profits. If the bank is responsible for the vehicle, you may have a future surprise coming. I have met many people who have dropped their vehicle off at the lease company and thought that was it. It was not until weeks later, after the bank had a chance to examine the vehicle, that they received a bill for what the bank hadn't considered "normal depreciation."

AutoSave Tip

Many car dealerships use more than one finance source for their leases and loans. They are not obligated to use the manufacturer's lending institution. Do not take it for granted that just because you are in a new car showroom, the dealership is going to use its manufacturer's finance source. Make sure you ask what source your dealership will be using to finance your lease or loan. Without any question, this can be the *most* important part of your satisfaction and will often determine the true nature, or overall cost, of the lease deal that you make.

Note: *Since this book was first introduced, I have continued to work within the automotive sales industry and I have also continued to research the shopping habits of consumers. During this research, I questioned consumers who were out shopping for a lease payment, asking them whom their previous lease payment quote was from. In other words, what financial institution was going to finance the quote that they received? The overwhelming majority of responses that I received was "What difference does it make; just give me your best quote?" Or when I did not receive that response, most of the rest simply told me that they didn't know or that they "presumed" it was from the manufacturer's financial source. I have to tell you that if there is nothing else you learn about leasing, this is without a doubt one of the biggest problems of why consumers have had, and continue to have, so many leasing "horror" stories. Would you let a doctor pick you? Would you let a lawyer pick you? Other than paying cash, when you purchase/lease an automobile you are just as importantly creating a relationship with the lending institution, not just the manufacturer or dealership. Did you know that some independent banks actually instruct their "lease-end inspectors" to average a certain dollar amount to charge you under the normal depreciation clause? Do you know that some banks actually pay their "lease-end inspectors" by commission, meaning the more they can make use of the normal depreciation clause, the more money they personally make? Hopefully, when and if the third edition of this book comes out, I will be able to "edit out" these statements. Maybe by then,*

---

laws will have been passed to prevent this form of "consumer abuse." But until then, I would like you to keep one very important thing in mind. Banks are in the business of selling paper (money) and automobile manufacturers financial sources are in the business of helping to sell more vehicles. Remember that not just a monthly payment determines the quality of a deal you get, or even determines the overall cost of that deal. For my money, at least until better laws are passed to protect consumers, I would stay with the automobile manufacturers' financial source for my lease, even if it doesn't offer me the lowest monthly payment!

Service. Independent lease companies rarely give you a choice of where they purchase your vehicle. Leasing companies buy from whomever gives them the best price. It is your problem how and where you get your vehicle serviced. Remember my definition of the "best deal" is a combination of service, convenience and price.

Making the deal. Independent lease companies can have an advantage here by making life a little easier. All you really have to do is walk into their offices and tell them what vehicle you want, and they will get the vehicle for you. You will not have to deal with the car dealership or car salesperson, they will—but at what cost to you?

Shopping and negotiating a lease

One major problem with shopping for a lease is that the lending laws of most states still do not require the selling price of the vehicle or the lease rate to be shown on the actual lease contract. Looking at it from the viewpoint of the automobile industry, I can understand why selling price is not shown. The customer is not actually purchasing the vehicle but simply paying for its depreciation for the time he or she uses it. I can also understand why lease rate is not shown. As explained earlier, lease rates and interest rates are not always the same thing, and most consumers could not amortize a lease, anyway.

From the consumer's viewpoint, however, I don't understand how such a growing alternative to conventional financing could be left with these major loopholes, thus offering the lessor a clear opportunity to deceive the consumer. (As stated previously, more financial institutions have volunteered to provide lease disclosure. Stay with someone who offers you this.)

Shopping price. If you deal with a lease contract that does not offer selling price disclosure, also referred to as capitalized cost, negotiating price is basically a waste of time.

If you find yourself in a situation in which you are looking to make a lease deal on a vehicle through a financial source that does not offer selling price disclosure, there are a couple of things you should do to help protect yourself. First, insist that an actual selling price, which the lease is based on, be written on your sales order. The next step, when you are comparison shopping, is to shop the overall cost of the lease. This should include the sum of the monthly payments plus the residual value, also referred to as the purchase option. You should question any other fees that may be applicable. Some lending institutions and lease companies have expensive lease filing and/or termination fees.

AutoSave Tip

Ask the salesperson to put the selling price in writing *before* he quotes you a monthly payment. If it is done afterwards, and the salesperson has already attempted a deception, he or she may choose to live with the gamble of writing down a false selling price rather than look for excuses for why the payment suddenly changed. Also, when you are ready to sign a lease contract that does include selling price disclosure, be sure to look at it! Sometimes dealerships and/ or salespeople will gamble that although they negotiated a selling price on a lease that does offer disclosure, you simply won't know where to look for the "cap cost" or simply won't bother to.

The reasoning behind having the salesperson write the selling price on your sales contract, even though it may not appear on your lease contract, is based on human nature: Fewer people will deceive you in writing than they would verbally!

Shopping rate. Because lease rates and actual interest rates are often two completely different numbers, do not use an advertised rate as your only guideline. (Because lease rates are not actual APRs, many states will not allow them to be advertised.) Although a lease rate, if calculated as an interest rate, will often turn out to be a higher figure, there is something to be said for the incentive programs that many automobile manufacturers offer. For example, even if a quoted lease rate of 2.9 actually equaled 6.9 percent interest, it doesn't mean that the lease is still not a good deal. The bottom line here is that the lease rate should not be a part of your comparison shopping. There are just too many other variables. Leave your shopping to looking at what kind of a monthly payment you can get, and keep in mind what the overall cost of the lease would be if you brought it full circle and either turned in the vehicle or purchased it. And please don't forget that you should be *very* concerned with whom you are considering borrowing the money from!

How to calculate the APR of a lease rate

There are reasons why a lease rate is not the same as an interest rate. As mentioned earlier, a lease rate may have other factors, not usually associated with an interest rate, built into it. For instance, a lease rate may include the cost of built-in GAP protection or a road-side assistance program offered by the manufacturer, and possibly other expenses incurred by the lender through its leasing program. But if you are simply one of those consumers who wishes to see what it is costing you to borrow in the form of an interest rate, the following example will be helpful. Just remember to keep in mind that the lease rate may include some additional benefits for you.

The example we will use is a vehicle that a dealership is allowing you to buy or lease for the selling price of $10,000. The dealership can conventionally finance the vehicle at a 10 percent interest rate. You will use no money down for either, but with the lease you will have a $3,000 purchase option.

The total cost of financing your purchase and of leasing it might be figured out in the following way:

> **Finance** $10,000 @ 10% for 48 months
> = $253.63 per month x 48 months
> = a total cost of $12,174.24

Lease quoted @ $210.00 per month x 48 months
= total payments of $10,080.00
+ your purchase option of $3,000
= a total cost of $13,080.00

Why did the lease in this example cost more? (In reality, in most cases it will not cost more. I simply felt that it was important to show you how other areas can determine your overall costs). There are three possible explanations for the $905.76 difference.

1. **Lease rate.** Although neither interest rate nor lease rate was quoted for the lease, the total figure tells us that the cost of borrowing the money equaled an approximate APR of 13.75 percent. This rate was figured by taking the $13,080 and dividing it by 48 months. It came to $272.50. By using the amortization tables in the back of this guide, the financed amount of $10,000 for 48 months came closest to the payment factor of .027201 (.027201 x 10,000 = 272.01). Looking to the left of the table, it revealed an APR of 13.75 percent.

2. **Actual selling price (cap cost).** There is the possibility that the dealership or salesperson quoted you one selling price but based the lease on a higher figure. This could be all of the $905.76 difference in itself or simply make up part of the difference, combined with the actual APR as explained above.

3. **Purchase option.** One of the easiest lease deceptions is the purchase option. Most consumers lease with the intention of walking away from the vehicle. This is, however, often not the case. For many different reasons, many consumers do end up "buying out" their leases. Because leases are usually sold by the amount of the monthly payment, few consumers take a good look at the amount of their purchase option. This offers the dealership the potential for extra profits down the road by quoting a purchase option higher than the actual residual value. This "packing of profit" can range from a few hundred dollars to as much as a few thousand dollars. Basically, the amount will be whatever the dealership can get away with. If you choose to walk away

from the vehicle, the dealership doesn't lose—it already made money leasing the vehicle to you to start with. However, if you purchase the vehicle, it means "found money" for the dealership. *Always* compare your lease-end purchase option on the contract to the contract's residual value. (They are almost always listed as two separate amounts) If there is more than a couple of hundred dollars difference, someone is setting you up for a *fall* should you decide in the future to exercise your purchase option. (Refer to "Terminating early or buying out a lease" on page 130 and "What to do before your lease ends" on page 133.)

I would estimate that I have seen more than 75 percent of vehicles leased with this extra profit added into the purchase option. If you are leasing now, you may be able to eliminate the extra profit that might be in your current lease contract.

Although I have used the phrases "residual value" and "purchase option" interchangeably, they are listed separately on most lease contracts.

Because it is difficult to know if I am leasing the vehicle for a higher price or interest rate than I was quoted, how do I shop?

First, as previously mentioned, get the dealership to put the selling price in writing. Few dealership or salespeople who may be inclined to quote one price and base the lease on a different one will do so if they have to put the actual selling price in writing.

Also, if you are not given an invoice (bill of sale), demand one! The invoice is a receipt that few consumers look at because they don't get it until after the deal is made or the vehicle has been delivered. It is usually stuffed in an envelope with copies of your contracts or motor vehicle papers. This invoice will show the actual selling price of the vehicle and should be compared to any figures that you were quoted and/or to the price you had them put in writing.

Some dealerships may not give you a bill of sale based on the fact that you are not actually purchasing the vehicle; the finance company giving you the lease is the actual purchaser. This is a valid point. Just remember though, someone who is not willing to give you a document that discloses the transaction you just made may be attempting to hide something.

When you are doing comparison shopping, be sure you get all the facts. As explained earlier, two different lending institutions offering the same lease rate may not be offering the same overall cost. In addition, many leases have filing and/or lease-end fees involved. These can be hundreds of dollars and should be used as a part of your comparison shopping. Always add up all of your costs and calculate one total figure on which to base your comparisons.

Always pay close attention to mileage guidelines and the cost of exceeding them. Many leases are advertised with very low yearly mileage allowances and very high excess mileage fees, in order to advertise a very low monthly payment. If you feel that you are going to exceed the mileage guideline, find out if including this in your contract is to your benefit. Most leasing companies charge less for excess mileage if you claim it up front, instead of at the end. On the other hand, if you are an individual who puts unusually low mileage on a vehicle, what was an advertising ploy to them may be a benefit to you.

AutoSave Tip

Some financial sources offer rebates for unused mileage in excess of their guidelines. For example, if a lease was normally based on 15,000 miles a year, and you had it written for 20,000 miles (with the extra mileage added into your monthly payment) and you ended up putting on only 18,000 miles, you may be entitled to a rebate of the per-mile fee you paid up front for the 2,000 miles per year that you didn't use.

Always ask about the lease conditions to which you may be subject. If you lease commercially and you put lettering on a vehicle, you may be required to pay to have it removed at lease-end. Also be sure to ask what costs may be involved with terminating your lease. It always pays to ask questions. In this case, it almost always costs you not to! Again, always look at everything with the entire picture in mind.

Terminating early or buying out a lease

Like conventional loans, a lease does not necessarily have to be carried out to full term. You usually have the same options of buying, selling or trading in your vehicle before the lease ends.

Although market conditions and the resale value of a particular vehicle will vary, you usually need to be at least three fourths of the way through a lease before you can consider disposing of your contract without any major financial loses. If you consider selling out of your lease by retailing your vehicle, you should be able to slash a few months off of the time period mentioned above, because retailing a vehicle will always get you more than trading it in.

How can you sell what you don't own?

In one sense, you can't—you must pay for it first. It's no different than a conventional loan. Once again, you are obligated to an amount, not a term. Let's say your lease buyout is $15,000 and you have someone interested in buying your vehicle for $16,000. (Lease buyout is the balance of your monthly payments, often minus unused interest, plus your lease-end purchase option and possible lease termination fees.) Simply give the bank its $15,000 and you have the right to keep the other $1,000 profit! This holds true whether you are selling the vehicle privately or trading it in to a dealership.

AutoSave Tip

It is important to understand your state's sales tax laws. Call the lending institution directly and ask them about how you should handle the sale of your leased vehicle. If the title must first be transferred to your name, you may have to pay sales tax on the full buyout figure. You are, in essence, purchasing the vehicle. Some lending institutions will give the title directly to your buyer. That way, only that person has to pay the sales tax. With the case of trading in your vehicle for a profit to a dealership, the dealership does not have to pay sales tax and neither do you.

How to get your lease payoff figure

This is the most important and often the most costly part of terminating a lease early! Whether you're buying out the vehicle for yourself, trading it in or selling it, this is where the dealership can really hurt you. In many cases, you are required to contact the dealership directly, not the lending institution, to get your lease payoff amount. The original intent of this practice was to give the dealership the opportunity to lease or sell you another vehicle. How it really works is often quite different. A dealership that has included a purchase option profit, as previously discussed, is going to keep that profit in your payoff figure. In fact, because an early payoff leaves more unknowns, dealerships will often boost this profit even further. It is like being caught between a rock and a hard place. You want to get rid of the vehicle, but you're left at the mercy of the dealership. This doesn't always have to be the case.

If you call the bank asking for a payoff figure, you may be told that you must contact the dealership for your payoff. However, if you write a letter requesting a payoff figure, most lending institutions are obligated to respond. This benefits you because the payoff figure the bank gives you in writing will be net, meaning that even if the contract you signed had a built-in purchase option profit, it will not be included in the figure the bank gives you. By handling the situation in this manner, you can pay off the bank directly, bypassing the dealership and its packed-in profit. You should proceed in this manner even if you are trading in the vehicle. Don't rely on the figure the dealership gives you—get the net payoff in writing from the bank before you look to trade, sell or buy your leased vehicle.

If the bank refuses to supply you with a payoff figure and you have to handle it through the dealership, be sure to examine your lease contract. Find where both the "residual value" and "purchase options" amounts are listed and compare the two. If the purchase option is greater than the residual value, the difference represents the packed-in profit the dealership is attempting to make. You should negotiate this difference with the dealership, and your negotiations should be based on eliminating this profit entirely.

Although many leasing laws and/or practices seem to be moving in the general direction of helping consumers, others occasionally move in the opposite direction. When I first started to write this book, the technique I described above worked in most cases. Today, I am sorry to state that some of the automobile lending institutions have put an end to this practice of writing in to get the net payoff figure. It seems that too many dealerships complained that they were losing their packed-in purchase option profits—profits to which they felt they were entitled because they got the consumer, usually unknowingly, to sign for them. All I can say is, I hope that by making you aware of this fact, together we will be able to make the necessary changes that are still required to ensure that we consumers are not taken advantage of.

The mileage and condition of your leased vehicle can affect only how much it is worth to sell or trade. When the lease is bought out, you are not responsible for any mileage or normal depreciation costs that would normally apply when terminating a lease.

Some financial institutions are willing to negotiate your lease-end purchase option or buyout figure, regardless of whether this figure is actually a net residual value. This is because financial institutions are not in the business of selling vehicles, and they have to consider the costs involved with getting rid of your vehicle should you choose to walk away from it. (Basically, they'll have to hire a towing company to take your vehicle from the dealership, then send it away to be auctioned off to other dealerships and more than likely have to pay a commission to the auction itself.) They are usually so anxious to *not* get the vehicle back that they will consider any reasonable offer. This can save you a tremendous amount of money whether you are looking to buy the vehicle for yourself or sell it privately.

Contact the bank by phone after you have received a net payoff figure by mail (if you were able to do so). This should be done six to eight weeks in advance of your lease-end. Tell the bank that you are interested in buying your vehicle, but that you feel the buyout is too high. Ask if it will accept an offer and how you can go about making it. In most cases, the bank will accept your offer and will request that you send it in writing. You can usually check an automotive wholesale guide or ask your personal bank or a local car dealership to find out the actual wholesale value of your vehicle. Then offer the lending at least a few hundred dollars lower than that figure. I have seen this technique work numerous times, and it has saved people hundreds, even thousands, of dollars. Once again, the bank is not in the business of disposing of your leased vehicle and will often be anxious to take you on as a partner, even if it means that you are going to make a profit from the transaction.

What to do before your lease ends

Lease termination is an area that worries many consumers. Never knowing for sure what is going to be considered "normal depreciation," they find that a lease is never really over until the final bill is paid.

The best way to avoid problems with the clause "normal depreciation" is by not turning in your vehicle. If the lease is paid off, the condition of the vehicle is irrelevant. This does not mean you have to buy the vehicle. If the mileage is too high or you're concerned with its condition, put it up for sale six to 10 weeks before the lease ends. Make use of the information in the previous section on how to get your payoff figure, and then sell the vehicle. Even if the condition or mileage of your vehicle is such that you can get only what you owe, you may be saving yourself from a large normal depreciation charge.

You should be aware that when you complete a lease, the vehicle is purchased by the car dealership in many cases. As far as the lending institution is concerned, this means that the purchase option has been exercised, and the lending institution will receive its money. When a purchase option is exercised, the mileage and normal depreciation clause of your lease contract does not come into play.

However, dealerships often use this situation as an opportunity to purchase a vehicle for its used car lot at a cheap price. For example, you turn in a vehicle that has a purchase option of $10,000. Maybe you exceeded the mileage guidelines of your lease and didn't exactly keep the vehicle in great shape. In other words, when the dealership inspects your vehicle, it lets you know that you have a bill for $1,000. Now let's say that even with the excess mileage and poor condition of your vehicle, its wholesale value is still $10,000. The dealership will take your $1,000, combine it with only $9,000 of its own and pay off the purchase option. In essence, with your help, it has purchased the vehicle for its used car lot for $1,000 less than the actual value of the vehicle.

The way to avoid this type of situation is to always bring your leased vehicle into the dealership at least a month before your lease is up. Have the dealership inspect it at that time. If it looks like you are going to have some charges, ask if the dealership is willing to purchase the vehicle from you when the lease is up—of course, for the full amount of your purchase option, if not more. Once again, if a purchase option is exercised, there are no excess mileage or depreciation fees involved.

AutoSave Tip

Having your vehicle inspected early may be the determining factor in whether you should attempt to sell it on your own or start negotiating to have the dealership purchase it. Good dealerships are often willing to take a look at your vehicle before your lease ends. Because a dealership is experienced with many lease terminations, ask yours about the condition of your vehicle and what areas you might have to be concerned about.

If the dealership is not willing to commit to your vehicle, say that you intend to offer it to other dealerships. If the dealership still doesn't show interest in the vehicle, then you should carry out your "threat." Bring the vehicle to other dealerships, new or used, and tell them that you wish to sell the vehicle and that they can have it on the date your lease is up. Tell them that the amount you want is equal to, or could be greater than, your purchase option. Of course, all this depends on the condition of your vehicle or how many excess miles you put on it. You may not be able to get the purchase option amount, but by using the technique above, you will almost always minimize your losses, if not even make a profit.

If you cannot sell the vehicle yourself for any reason, prepare it for the lease-end inspection. Starting with the basics, make sure it's clean inside and out. Remember that many lease-end inspections result in reasons to charge you money. If there is any damage on the vehicle, whether minor dings, scratches or dents, get an independent estimate of the cost to repair it. You may even wish to take a few close-up photographs of your vehicle in the event of a dispute later on. (This should especially be done if the terms of your lease contract do not offer you a lease-end inspection report. In other words, some form of written proof as to the condition of the vehicle when you dropped it off at the dealership). If it needs any mechanical work, including items such as tires or brakes, find out how much they will cost you to replace or repair. Turning in your vehicle at lease-end should be viewed the same way as trying to sell it yourself or determining its trade-in value, as discussed in previous sections.

AutoSave Tip

Even if your vehicle is in great condition and you are not worried about the lease-end inspection, you should still see what it is worth in the marketplace and what it would cost to buy out the lease. If the vehicle is worth more than the buyout figure, why shouldn't *you* get the profit instead of the dealership or the bank? Even a quick sale at below-average retail can often put hundreds of dollars back into your pocket.

What if you can't make your payment(s)?

Regardless of how you choose to finance your purchase, circumstances in which you cannot meet your obligations may arise. Other than personal or medical problems, one of the major reasons consumers are not able to make their car payments is that they never created a proper budget in the first place. Refer to the section "Establishing a budget" on page 38 in Chapter 2.

I have seen numerous vehicles needlessly repossessed just because customers were afraid or embarrassed to admit they could not make their payments. Better a little embarrassment than a ruined credit rating. Again, even if a vehicle is worth a lot more than you still owe, it is a great expense of both time and money for the lender to take and dispose of it. (This is true for any kind of debt you may have.) Keep in touch with the lender. Let it know what your problems are. If a lender hears from you, it is very likely to work out alternatives. Many kinds of arrangements can be made, including postponement of some of your payments. Only when a lender does not hear from you does it begin to think you simply don't care.

If you know you will no longer be able to make any payments, or that the arrangements offered to you are still beyond your resources, try to sell the vehicle yourself. Find out your net payoff amount, and attempt to sell the vehicle for as close to that amount as possible. If you are out of equity, you may have to come up with some cash. This is better than ruining your credit rating, and the amount will usually be less than the bill you will receive from the bank for the difference between what you owed and the amount for which the bank sold the vehicle. Again, even if the obligation you can't meet is the new repayment schedule that you made with the lender, keep in touch. You may be surprised at just how far it will go to help you.

Many consumers have the misunderstanding that a voluntary repossession is somehow better than a repossession that was imposed upon them. To my knowledge, there is no difference between the two. All the banks I have ever dealt with viewed both types of repossession the same way when evaluating a person's credit history. Through voluntary repossession, you may be making it easier for the lender, but you are not making it easier for yourself. The only thing a voluntary repossession may give you is a lack of surprise when your vehicle is taken away.

Summary

You have just finished reading the largest and most complex section of this book. Some of you may feel more confused about leasing now than you did before you started. I apologize if the numerous ins and outs of leasing may have left you feeling that leasing is still one means of financing you don't wish to pursue.

For a simpler, more basic explanation of what leasing is all about, consider the following:

1. In its most basic form, leasing is really nothing more than a creative way of financing. All you are really doing is taking a portion of the cost of a vehicle, deferring it to a lease-end purchase option and giving yourself the opportunity to decide whether or not you wish to pay for the entire vehicle a few years later. The key word is option, meaning choice.

2. None of us are fortune-tellers. We can't predict the value of our vehicle two or three years from now. With leasing, you put the burden of being a fortune-teller on the automobile manufacturer or the lending institution giving you the lease. Again, you are simply given the option of whether or not you wish to pay for the entire vehicle a few years down the road. If the guess is wrong it's someone else's loss, not yours. (Remember that basically, a lease-end purchase option simply represents the amount of the vehicle that you never paid for to start with.)

3. Leasing rarely costs more than conventional financing and, in most cases, will cost less. As I have previously stated, if the overall cost of a lease is more than the overall cost of a conventionally financed purchase, odds are that someone is attempting to sell you a bad lease deal.

4. There are no "penalties" or "restrictions" with a lease. There are only guidelines that can be worked with or worked around.

By now, you have probably realized that I am a firm believer in leasing. My experience has shown me that most people who don't consider leasing don't consider it for three reasons. Either they had a bad experience with it in the past, they know someone else who had a bad experience or they are simply afraid of trying something new and creative that they don't understand. Don't let these reasons stop you from making an educated decision. You may wish to reread this chapter on leasing a few times to really get a grasp of all of the information I have given you. The key is not to look for what is bad about leasing, but to understand all of the good it has to offer. Odds are that leasing an automobile is going to be in your future, whether now, next year or a few years from now. Either that, or the way sticker prices are going, you will be considering a mortgage on your next automotive purchase!

What new rules should you have learned from this section?

1. Automobile manufacturers and dealerships are doing everything possible to sell you on leasing. They are doing this to increase their sales by offering you a way to keep your vehicle for a shorter period of time. In their efforts to accomplish this, however, they are also offering you a viable alternative to financing that you should be considering.

2. People consider or don't consider leasing for numerous reasons, but the fact is leasing is not what it used to be. You possibly only hurt yourself when you don't at least look at and understand what it is you may be saying no to.

3. In its most basic form, leasing has no penalties or restrictions. If this does not seem clear at this point, I strongly suggest that you reread the entire section on leasing.

4. There is no question that, in almost every case, an automobile manufacturer's financial source is the best place to acquire your lease.

5. As with all forms of purchasing, shopping for and negotiating a lease still requires you to keep in mind the "big picture," especially when considering whom and through whom you make your purchase.

The bottom line is that regardless of who you are or what you use your vehicle for, odds are that leasing is the way to go. I attempted to make leasing as simple as possible to understand, but there still might be some confusion. Reread this chapter as often as it takes. The reality of the situation is that if consumers really understood leasing, almost everyone would be doing it. Remember, cars are a depreciating product, not a commodity you want to own. The only way to win is to learn how to cut your losses! And what could be better than placing the burden of responsibility for what the future value of a product is going to be than on the people who built it or sold it to you to start with!

Chapter 6

Dealer
"after-sell"

About dealer "after-sell" products

After-sell, a part of dealerships' "back-end" sales efforts, is one of their largest profit areas. It consists of any product that is sold in addition to your vehicle. It includes items such as rust-proofing, fabric guard, door-edge guards, extended warranties, alarms and any other item from which a dealership can make money. Like every aspect of automobile sales, the underlying rule for the dealership is "you can always come down in price, but it's tough to go back up." Simply stated, these products are usually marked up with very high profit margins and are all negotiable.

Some of these products do offer you value, but many don't. Their value, or lack thereof, is discussed later in this section. Again, the key is to *buy* something rather have it *sold* to you. Buying a vehicle is a big step for most people, and when the deal is made, you are usually feeling very excited and protective about your purchase. This is why the dealership usually waits until after you have placed your deposit on the vehicle to introduce you to the person who is going to try to sell you these "after-sell" items. It is also why these items are often marketed in product groups as "protection packages." What could be a better time to try to sell them to you than right after you have made your purchase?

I've known dealerships that sold rust-proofing but never applied it to the vehicle. They get away with this because few of today's vehicles have rust problems. Some dealerships use this form of deception with extended warranties and other types of after-sell products; they'll sell you a policy but never register it. Some dealerships justify such deception by creating trust funds with some of the profit to handle any future claims. This may justify it in their minds, but the bottom line is that it is still a deception. Keep in mind, too, that guarantees on after-sell items are only as good as the company that is supplying them.

Dealerships always attempt to deliver a vehicle as soon as possible after a deal has been made. Their primary concern is what is known as "buyer's remorse." They know that the longer you wait to take delivery of your vehicle, the more likely you are to decide to "back out" of the deal or discover a deception they have gotten away with so far.

"Buyer's remorse" is causing more and more dealerships to implement a policy of "spot" deliveries. In other words, they want you to take the vehicle at the time you purchase it to eliminate the possibility of changing your mind about the vehicle or any product you may have purchased along with it.

AutoSave Tip

You should allow 48 to 72 hours between the time you purchase your vehicle and the time you call to schedule its pickup. Some of the initial excitement will have worn off, and you will be in a much better position to evaluate your decisions. Tell the dealership not to apply or install any of the products you have purchased until you have called back with your permission. Do not have any of these items listed on your sales contract until you have authorized them. Also, do not accept verbal guarantees of any kind. Make sure they are in writing and backed by a well-established company!

If you choose to make a change in your vehicle, such as upgrading an AM/FM stereo to a cassette, make sure you know the brand being used and who is going to make the change. Few dealerships use factory products to perform this type of upgrade because of their cost. There are companies that build "look-a-likes" at much cheaper prices. If you have a problem with a look-a-like product later on, your dealership may not be willing to take care of it. It may simply refer you to the company that did the work. This could turn out to be quite an inconvenience for you. This is true for many after-market products. Items such as sunroofs, luggage racks and air conditioning are often sent out by the dealership to outside companies that actually perform the installation of these products.

Extended warranties

Like many forms of insurance, extended warranties are a gamble. If you never use the insurance, you complain about its cost. If you use it, you rave about its value. The feature I like most about extended warranties is the budget control. They can eliminate the sudden unexpected repair bill and lower it to nothing more than the warranty's deductible. Unlike most after-sell products, warranties can be very confusing. They offer a wide variety of conditions and terms. Because they do vary so much, there is no way I can list an actual dollar amount that you should pay for them. What I can do is help you pick out the right one.

AutoSave Tip

Dealerships always have a price list from the company that supplies the warranty. They may not show you their cost, but you should ask to see their suggested retail price list. This is the price from which you should start your negotiating, not the verbal asking price that the dealership's representative offers you, a price that is usually considerably higher than it should be. (Be wary of prices or monthly payments that seem ridiculously low. Remember that dealerships often pre-sell you items by packing them into a payment they quoted you before they even started to try to sell these items to you.) Also, if a dealership will not show you the price list for the warranty, you can almost always check with the company that is providing it and find out how much they suggest the retail price should be.

What to look for in an extended warranty

Supplier. Not all extended warranties are from the automobile manufacturer. Many independent companies offer warranties to dealerships, often for a lower cost. What can this mean for you? A manufacturer's warranty is good at any of its dealerships and usually requires little or no cash outlay from you. Independent warranty companies may require you to have repairs done only by a dealership that handles their policy. They may require you to pay for the repairs up front and then wait to be reimbursed at a later time.

Coverage. Dealerships often try to sell only the best, most expensive warranty. There are always alternatives. Look at the options on your vehicle and compare them to what the warranty covers. If it covers a lot more options than you have, then you are looking at the wrong warranty. Most basic vehicles, with few options, need little or no extra coverage. Luxury cars, on the other hand, may need a lot.

Mileage and term. Many different warranty terms are usually available. Consider your driving habits. Estimate how many miles a year you drive and for how long you will probably keep your vehicle. If you drive 25,000 miles a year, a five-year, 50,000 mile warranty is not ideal for you. A three-year, 75,000 mile warranty would better fit your needs. If a longer term doesn't cost too much extra, you may wish to consider it for increasing the resale value of your vehicle. Most warranties are transferable for a nominal fee, and they can increase the resale value of your vehicle, while making it much easier to sell.

Deductibles. Deductibles will affect the cost of your warranty. Ask how much you might save by increasing your deductible.

AutoSave Tip

If you no longer have your vehicle before the term of the extended warranty ends, you can usually send in a cancellation form and receive a prorated refund for the unused portion. This should be kept in mind if your vehicle is stolen or totaled in an accident.

Everything seems to happen after the warranty ends. Make use of it while you can. If the warranty is coming to an end, have a mechanic give your vehicle a thorough checkout. Many things that can lead to a breakdown don't always happen overnight. A small investment in having your vehicle checked out might help you find a problem that could cost you a lot more money in the future, after the warranty has ended.

Antitheft systems

Auto theft has been, is and will continue to be, a big business. Consumers often mistakenly think that they don't need protection because they live in a "nice" area. Vehicles are rarely stolen from homes.

Shopping malls, movie theaters and any other places that have parking lots and crowds of people have the highest theft rates.

Antitheft devices can range from $25 to $1,000. Part of their cost may be covered by insurance discounts. Check with your insurance agent about what kind of discounts are available and for what type of device. Most insurance companies look for a "passive" system. This is any device that can arm itself automatically. In other words, it's not up to you to remember to turn it on.

AutoSave Tip

Most dealerships mark up a security system by 100 percent of its total cost. You should be able to negotiate at least 20 percent off. You will usually find your best deal and variety of choices with outside independent companies. Many car stereo stores specialize in automobile security systems, or you can simply look in the telephone directory yellow pages.

Systems with audible sirens are fine but should be accompanied by an ignition-kill device or by some other means of mechanical or physical theft prevention. In cities and most suburban areas, the sound of car alarms going off is so common that few people bother to pay attention to them anymore. In many cases, when a car alarm sounds, it is not because the vehicle is being stolen but because the alarm's sensitive motion detector has been set off by the wind or by someone coming into contact with the vehicle. Most professional thieves can disarm a siren within moments after it has gone off.

Today, most car thieves are professionals, not kids looking for a joy ride. Do not put a sticker on your vehicle that advertises what type of security system you have installed. By doing this, you are telling the thief what he needs to know to bypass or disable it. A generic sticker stating only that the vehicle is protected is the best kind. Any device that uses the same installation method on all vehicles, such as a factory-installed system, also offers little protection against the professional thief. Your local police department or auto club can offer you good recommendations on the most effective systems.

Chemicals and miscellaneous "after-sell"

The product list that follows often represents more of a profit to the dealership than the sale of the vehicle itself. Although labor rates have recently skyrocketed, affecting the dealerships' cost to install these products, this increase in labor costs only puts a small dent into their profit margins. Many of these products are sold for 10 times what they cost the dealership.

Remember, a dealership will usually attempt to sell you these products right after you have bought your vehicle. This is when you are feeling the most protective about your purchase. Don't be sold by impulse; use your shopping list and once again, give yourself some time to think about any purchase that you may make.

AutoSave Tip

Beware of "protection packages." Many dealerships will group products together, such as rust-proofing, undercoating and paint sealant. They will highly inflate their individual prices and then show you a large discount if you purchase the whole package. Buy what you want, but negotiate each item separately.

Most of the following products come with some form of warranty or guarantee. Make sure you get a copy of it and understand all of its terms. It should be noted here that many states define the actual term of a lifetime warranty differently. If a product is being offered to you with a lifetime warranty, ask how its term is defined. Many after-sell product warranties also specify conditions or inspection clauses that you must maintain in order to keep your coverage valid. You should check them out thoroughly because many of the conditions are written in the hopes that your noncompliance will give the dealership the opportunity to invalidate a claim.

Although costs and retail prices for the items listed on the following pages vary between dealerships and geographic areas, the information presented is from my personal experience, showing what I feel is the most you should pay for these products.

Rust-proofing. This is when the inside surface of your vehicle's sheet metal is treated with a chemical designed to inhibit rust. Usually, holes are drilled to gain access, the chemical is sprayed inside and then the holes are capped.

>Average retail price: $200-$500
>Average dealer cost: $35-$75
>The most that you should pay: $200

Most vehicles today have long-term factory warranties against rust. Buying rust-proofing today is little more than attempting to better the warranty you already get from the automobile manufacturer for free. The only time you should consider buying rust-proofing is when you are not satisfied with the manufacturer's warranty or if you live in an area where roads are salted often and you plan on keeping your vehicle for a very long time.

Undercoating. Generally referred to today as "sound shielding," this feature involves spraying the undercarriage of your vehicle with a tar-like substance.

>Average retail price: $75-$200
>Average dealer cost: $35-$50
>The most that you should pay: $75

Undercoating will do little more than possibly help your vehicle ride more quietly. Spray cans of undercoating can be bought in most automotive parts stores, and you can apply it yourself for $10 to $20.

Paint sealant. This is the application of a wax-like substance designed to protect the paint finish of your vehicle.

>Average retail price: $150-$400
>Average dealer cost: $30-$75
>The most that you should pay: $150

Many paint sealants are nothing more than a decent coating of wax. Many of today's vehicles already come with a factory "clearcoat" finish. A good regular wax job with most store-bought waxes will do the same thing that most paint sealants do. Some new products on the market, however, are specifically designed to help protect a vehicle against "acid rain." Acid rain is a growing problem. If this is a product you do consider, remember that the product is only as good as the warranty backing it.

Fabric guard. This is the application of a stain resistant chemical to the interior fabric of your automobile.

> Average retail price: $100-$300
> Average dealer cost: $15-$35
> The most that you should pay: $75

Some automobile manufacturers have started offering some of their products with factory pretreated fabric. Many of these products are fine until you clean up a spot. This usually removes the chemical treatment along with the spot. Most supermarkets sell spray cans of fabric protector for under $10.

AutoSave Tip

Items such as pinstripes, door-edge guards and other appearance products usually have the highest markup. You should start by offering the dealer one-quarter to one-half of the asking price. Many of these products are easy to apply and can be purchased inexpensively at most automotive parts stores.

To help raise profits, dealerships often install some of these products on their in-stock vehicles and then add a dealer "add-on" sticker to the vehicle. If the vehicle you want already has these products with it, you should negotiate these prices separately. It should also be noted that just because a vehicle has an "add-on" label showing a charge for a particular dealer-installed item, it does not mean that the item has already been installed. More can be read in "Dealer add-on labels" on page 70 in Chapter 3.

Summary

Dealer after-sell represents a part of the "back-end" profits a dealership makes on the sale of a vehicle. These profits, as previously mentioned, often represent two-thirds of the overall profit a dealership will make on the sale.

What new rules should you have learned from this section?

1. Although after-sell is a high-profit area for the dealership, some of the products mentioned, if purchased for the right price, can help to protect your investment or increase your overall satisfaction with your new vehicle.

2. Be leery of after-sell "packages." When a dealership groups the products it is attempting to sell, it will usually highly inflate the individual prices of each item to show a greater package discount.

3. Out of all the many after-sell products that are sold, an extended warranty, in most cases, should be an item that you consider. Just remember to follow my guidelines and purchase the right one for the right price.

Chapter 7

Buying a used vehicle

Can someone else's headache be your good deal?

The heading for this section is probably the one question that has prevented more people from considering a used vehicle than any other.

With new vehicle sticker prices becoming out of reach for many consumers, used vehicles have been all but forced into becoming a consideration. Late-model used vehicles can be an excellent value, but only when the "big picture" is first considered. If it isn't, used vehicles can often end up costing more than new vehicles in the long run, and not just because of repairs. "The economics of a used vehicle purchase" on page 151 will further explain this.

Used vehicles are generally purchased through one of three different sources. You will either buy them privately or from a new or used car dealership. All three have their individual advantages and disadvantages. Once again, the reliability and reputation of whom you do business with will be the keys to your satisfaction.

From whom should you buy a used vehicle? Consider the following before you decide:

A private owner. This is the person from whom you can usually get the best price but will also have the least amount of recourse. Buying privately usually means buying a vehicle "as is." This means not getting any kind of warranty with the vehicle.

You should be aware that, since the early 1990s, most new vehicle warranties have gone with the vehicle, not the owner. If you are considering a late-model used vehicle, you should contact a local dealer and supply the vehicle's identification number (V.I.N.), and the dealership should be able to tell you what, if any, manufacturer's warranty is still left on the vehicle and if it is available to you as the new owner.

Used car dealer. Used car dealership prices are usually higher than buying privately but lower than buying from a new car dealership. Used car dealerships come and go and have always had the worst reputation among car dealerships. Sales tactics such as turning back odometers and hiding physical or mechanical damage are not that uncommon. This is not to say that all used car dealerships are bad. Some do have a good reputation and will offer good values. As you would with new car dealerships, you should make an inquiry to your local Better Business Bureau before you decide to shop. Unlike a private seller, a reputable used car dealership will usually check a vehicle out and offer it with some kind of warranty.

New car dealer. This is where you will usually pay top dollar for a used vehicle, but it is also where you may be getting the "best" overall "deal." New car franchises' reputations are more important to them. New car dealerships are usually more anxious to earn your repeat business, making them more concerned with your overall satisfaction. Many late-model vehicles they sell are purchased from auctions that only members from new car dealerships can attend. The dealership is usually required to do a complete mechanical inspection on these vehicles before offering them for sale. Some late-model vehicles they sell often have the remaining balance of the new vehicle warranty.

As just mentioned, many of the vehicles on a new car dealership's used car lot are often purchased at special auctions. Many of these vehicles are called "program" cars. Odds are that if you have ever shopped for a used vehicle at a new car dealership, or have read its advertising, you are already aware of the term "program car." A program vehicle is one that has already been titled, but by the automobile manufacturer or its finance source. Some of these vehicles may have been short-term leases or vehicles actually driven by the manufacturer's employees. Others may have been part of a rental fleet such as Hertz or Avis.

Where a vehicle has come from is not as important as its current condition and the warranty being offered with it. In the past, many consumers had negative emotions about purchasing vehicles that were once owned by a rental car company. The fact is, most rental car companies follow better routine maintenance schedules than most consumers do. Don't let where a "program" vehicle may have come from dissuade you from considering it as a good alternative to a new car.

The economics of a used vehicle purchase

The first two years of a new vehicle are when it takes its quickest loss in value, often about one-third of its original selling price. This can make the selling price of a model that is one or two years old look very enticing, but the selling price is not your only expense. The cost of maintenance and financing can outweigh what seemed originally to be a good deal. This is not to say that used vehicles don't have economic advantages. Based on the same selling price, a used vehicle will offer you a lot more options for the money. This is one of the primary reasons people buy used.

As an example, we will consider that you are comparing two vehicles valued at $12,000 each. One is new, and one is two model years old with 24,000 miles on it. You have $2,000 to apply as a down payment and you are looking to finance the balance for 48 months. Because the two-model-year-old vehicle has the same selling price as the new one, for the purpose of this example, we will figure that it originally had a selling price of $16,000. The used car is also more of a luxurious car than can be afforded new.

Let's first take a look at some of the expenses from which you are usually free for the first couple of years with a new vehicle, but which are expense considerations for a used one:

Brakes. Usually good for 15,000 to 30,000 miles, depending on your driving habits. Unless they have recently been replaced, they will soon be an expense.

Tires. Usually good for around 40,000 miles. At 24,000 miles, they will still look okay, but their life is more than half over.

Tune-ups. Average about every 35,000 miles. You will probably need a tune-up within your first year of ownership.

Warranties. Even if the vehicle has the balance of a new vehicle warranty, that balance will usually only cover the power train. Better coverage for items such as air conditioning and power windows, which are covered with a new vehicle purchase, will have to be purchased again for a used vehicle. Expect the cost to be between $400 and $800.

Financing. This may be the biggest expense. Few banks offer to finance used vehicles for the same interest rate as new ones. Expect to pay at least 2 percent to 5 percent higher for used. That gap can be 10 percent or higher when new vehicle incentive programs come into play.

Let's take a look at an example of the possible difference between financing a new vehicle and a used one. (Example is based on financing the $10,000 balance for the $12,000 vehicle described previously, for which you intend on putting $2,000 down.)

New: $10,000 for 48 months @ 7.9 = $243.66 a month
Total loan cost: $11,695.68 + $2,000 down payment =$13,695.68

Used: $10,000 for 48 months @12.5 = $265.80 month
Total loan cost: $12,758.40 + $2,000 down payment =$14,758.40

You just spent $1,062.72 more in interest to borrow the same $10,000. Now add in the cost of purchasing a warranty and almost immediate maintenance expenses, and the gap grows even larger. These points are not meant to steer you away from used vehicles. Remember, if the used vehicle originally sold for $16,000 two years ago, you are most likely getting a better-equipped vehicle than the new vehicle. The expenses shown here are just a reminder to keep the "big picture" in mind and to show you just what these extra options in the used vehicle are actually costing you.

Buying a used vehicle from a dealership

Most of us think of buying a used vehicle as a gamble. We ask ourselves: *Did I get a good deal? Does the vehicle have problems I don't know about?* As with any form of gambling, the more the odds are on your side, the better chance you have to win. With used vehicles, the odds are in your favor if you know how to shop and what to look for.

Shopping. Whom you buy from is probably never as important as it is with the purchase of a used vehicle. The same price guides and techniques discussed in the section "The 'four market values' of your current vehicle" on page 44 in Chapter 2 should be used here. Unlike new vehicles, in which prices are set by the manufacturer, used vehicles are sold for whatever the market will bear. Used car dealerships usually work with smaller profit margins in their efforts to be competitive with new car dealerships.

If you don't have an idea of the actual value of the vehicle you are considering, even a tremendous discount doesn't guarantee that you are getting a good deal. My experience has shown that at new car dealerships, most used vehicles are marked up $2,000 to $4,000 more than the dealer's cost. The cost usually includes what the dealership has spent to recondition the vehicle. The more the vehicle is worth, the higher the markup.

What should you be looking for?

A used car lot is no different than any other kind of display advertising: Make the product look good and you are going to have customers. Keep in mind that a vehicle's value is a lot more than skin deep.

Outside view. Take a good look at the vehicle from different angles and, if possible, under different lighting. In most cases, even excellently done body work will be evident. Even the best paint job will show signs of over-spray. If body work has been done, not only might you see different color shades but, almost always, slight ripples. These are best seen from front to back, or from back to front if you're in a crouched-down position. Few body shops take a vehicle apart to repaint a damaged area. Take a close look at body-side molding, trim molding and window molding. Paint over-spray is usually pretty obvious. Take a head-on look at the car's tires. Uneven wear can be a sign of trouble. Examine the windshield for small cracks or star-breaks. These may lead to windshield replacement.

Inside view. Open and close the doors and look at how they line up. Open the hood and the trunk and look inside where the body parts come together. It is usually obvious, even for the untrained eye, to see if body panels have been replaced or patched. Check the interior for rips and burns. Take a close look at the odometer and see how the numbers line up. If they are crooked or unevenly spaced, it may be a sign that the mileage has been tampered with.

AutoSave Tip

If you are unsure of damage you discover but you like the vehicle, invest a little to have a professional auto body person take a look at it. Many vehicles have had minor damage repaired that will have nothing to do with the satisfaction or reliability of your purchase. Also, just as dealerships do when they find faults with your trade-in, tell the dealership that the minor damage you discover bothers you, even if it doesn't. This is one of your negotiating tools.

Mechanical. Regardless of the warranty being offered, always have the vehicle checked out by a mechanic before you commit to it.

Some dealerships allow you to hold the vehicle with a deposit until it can be checked out. Make sure that your deposit is refundable. If you follow this procedure, dealerships will often fix problems they are aware of before your mechanic gets a chance to see them. A good mechanic often finds problems that may soon be an expense, even if they are not now. Anything your mechanic finds, no matter how minor, is an additional negotiating tool for you when you start to discuss price with the dealership.

If, for whatever reason, you end up buying a used vehicle without a mechanic looking at it first, have it checked out right after buying it.

4 x 4s (four-wheel-drive vehicles). In most cases, a good look under the vehicle will tell you about its off-road experience. Scratches and caked-on dirt are sure signs that it has been used off-road. If it has, have the front end, four-wheel-drive transfer case and suspension checked out professionally before you make your purchase decision.

Buying a used vehicle privately

What you've read so far about buying from a dealership should be applied to buying privately. Here are a few extra tips regarding a private purchase:

1. Buying privately usually means no guarantees of any kind. If a seller offers you one, make sure that you get it in writing and, if possible, have a witness cosign it.

2. Ask for identification from the seller and compare that to the name on the title.

3. Be sure that you see the title before you give the seller any money. A lost title can take months to replace, and you will not be able to register the vehicle until the new title arrives.

4. If a person still owes money on his or her vehicle, make that portion of your buying price payable to the lender. If possible, accompany the seller to the lien holder and request that the title be turned over to you.

5. Always have the vehicle checked out by a mechanic.

6. Check the V.I.N. listed on the title against the one on the vehicle. This number can be found in the lower corner of the dashboard on the driver's side and viewed from the outside through the windshield.

AutoSave Tip

Be wary of vehicles that have had engines rebuilt or replaced, even if documentation can be provided to prove it, remember that the rest of the vehicle has still taken the wear and tear of the overall mileage. Also, if someone claims to be selling you a "one owner" vehicle, check it out. There are codes on the title that can tell you whether this is true or not. Your local motor vehicle agency can tell you where they are and what they mean.

As previously stated, you may often get the "best price" through a private purchase, but remember that there is little or no recourse for you against the seller if a problem arises.

Leasing a used vehicle

Based on the popularity of short-term new vehicle leasing, most dealerships have found their used car lots filled with late model, often high-priced used vehicles. Because these late-model vehicles are often outside the financial reach of many buyers, the idea of leasing used vehicles came into being just a short time ago. Pretty much everything you have read about new-vehicle leasing holds true with used vehicles with one major exception: Few consumers out shopping for a used vehicle compare the costs to that of a new one. Be very careful! What may seem like a great alternative to financing a used vehicle can often cost as much or even more than the monthly payment to lease that same vehicle brand new. As I have previously stated, if you are going to make yourself the best possible deal, always explore and weigh-all of the alternatives. If after doing this you find that the lease being offered on the used vehicle really is a good deal, congratulate yourself on being an educated consumer, one who checked out all the possibilities and made an informed and financially creative decision.

Used vehicle warranties

Many states require dealerships to warranty all of their used vehicles. Some states allow vehicles to be sold "as is." This is about the same as buying a vehicle privately. An "as is" sale doesn't necessarily mean the vehicle is bad. Some vehicles simply don't have enough value for the dealership to bother investing in them.

AutoSave Tip

Many owners are not aware that the balance of their original factory warranty can be transferred to a new owner. Look in the back of the owner's manual or warranty book. It will tell you if the warranty is transferable and, if so, for how much. If these books are not available, you can check with your local dealership, which can input the serial number of the vehicle into a computer and tell you what coverage may still remain. In some cases, you can even get a repair history on the vehicle. This also holds true with most extended warranties.

The most important part of a warranty is not its term but what it covers for what cost. Most warranties have deductibles of $25 to $200 and are designed to share the cost of repairs with the consumer. Some cover parts but not labor. Some cover both, but at a percentage. The most common is 50/50: You pay half, the dealership pays half. This type is usually not fair because the work is done for whatever amount it costs the dealer. For you, it is closer to an 80/20 split.

Never take the word of a dealership or salesperson when a guarantee to take care of something is offered. Make sure that you get everything in writing. Most used car and new car dealerships have a standard warranty that they offer with their used vehicles. They can range anywhere from 30 days to two years and will vary as to the extent of their coverage. The dealerships that offer the longer warranties usually just "pack" them into the price of the vehicle. They use this packed-in warranty to make you believe that they are willing to back their products better than their competitors. They are successful at doing this because you can rarely shop and compare the prices of two identical used vehicles the way you can with new vehicles that come with the manufacturer's price sticker.

AutoSave Tip

If you have had a vehicle thoroughly checked out by an independent mechanic and the results are good, you may wish to discuss eliminating all or part of the warranty the dealership is offering with the vehicle when you negotiate the price. Most dealerships consider "substantial added discounts" on a vehicle's price if they can reduce their warranty responsibility.

If you intend to use the suggestion previously mentioned, be sure you are confident about the mechanical inspection you had. In most cases, I recommend warranties. The previously mentioned tip was only given as an alternative to lowering the purchase price of the vehicle.

What are the basic types of used vehicle warranties?

State inspection. The dealership guarantees that your vehicle will pass your state's motor vehicle inspection requirements. In most states, the dealership is required to cover 100 percent of the repairs for any item that does not pass.

Power train. Power train components make up the engine, transmission and drive axle. This coverage can be misleading. Items such as fuel injectors may be on the engine but are not considered part of the power train. Have the warranty explained to you and be sure that you understand what percentage of coverage you are offered and for what components.

High-tech. This type of warranty has different levels of coverage. Some cover a few extras such as air conditioning, electrical system and so forth, while others cover almost every component, except for normal wear and tear on items such as tires, brake pads, belts and so on.

New vehicle warranty. Many late-model used vehicles may still have the balance of the original factory warranty. This coverage may cost you nothing or just a small transfer fee. Ask the dealership what the balance of the warranty covers and for how long. It may not volunteer this information on its own, since it wants to sell you a warranty.

Be leery of used vehicles that supposedly have the balance of the manufacturer's warranty. For example, the emissions system on most new vehicles is warrantied longer than the rest of the vehicle. If the rest of the vehicle is out of warranty, but the emissions system is still covered, a dealership can put a sticker on the vehicle stating that it is covered by the balance of the original manufacturer's warranty. Of course, this leads people to believe more is covered than actually is.

Make sure you know who is backing your warranty as well as what your responsibilities are to maintain it. Three sources usually back warranties:

Dealership. Also known as an "in-house warranty," this type of coverage is offered by the dealerships themselves. In most cases, if you have any problems, you will have to bring the vehicle back to the dealership from which you bought it. This can be an inconvenience unless you happen to break down or have a problem near that dealership. Many dealerships can supply those who travel with national listings of their franchises, showing locations and telephone numbers of where to get service. Of course, this type of warranty is only as good as the dealership's reputation and only good for as long as the dealership is still in business.

Independents. Many outside companies sell warranty policies to dealerships which in turn sell them to you. Many require that you have the work performed only after their approval and only at certain locations. With this type of warranty, you will usually have to lay out the money yourself and wait to be reimbursed. Although most outside independent warranties are found at used car dealers because they are not associated with automobile manufacturers, many new car dealers also make use of them. This is because these warranties are usually cheaper for the dealership to purchase than those offered by the manufacturer. As with most things, you usually get what you pay for. These warranties are usually more difficult to make use of and will cover fewer components.

AutoSave Tip

Always make sure you get a warranty registration card or form that has been signed by someone in dealership management. If you are financing your warranty with the rest of the vehicle, be sure the warranty is listed on the finance contract. Verify the warranty terms on the form against what you were told you were purchasing. Make sure your V.I.N. is listed on the warranty and check it against the V.I.N. on the vehicle you purchased. In most cases, when a dealership sends in your warranty registration, you will be notified by the company backing it that they have received it. If you do not receive notification within six to eight weeks from the time you purchased the warranty, contact the dealership or the warranty company directly and verify that your warranty is valid!

Manufacturer. Whether it is the balance of a factory warranty or a policy sold by the dealership, coverage that is backed by the manufacturer is usually the best kind. For these warranties, you rarely have to pay money up front, and you usually can have the work done at any of the manufacturer's dealers in North America. Although these warranties may cost a bit more, remember, the manufacturers are looking for your repeat business and are generally much easier to deal with.

Certified used vehicles

In recent years, many automobile manufacturers, and even some outside companies, have begun to sign up dealerships to participate in used vehicle certification programs. These programs usually require that a used vehicle receive a very extensive mechanical checkout. If the vehicle passes, or is repaired to the point of meeting the certification standards, the vehicle is then specially marked on a dealership's lot as a "Certified Used Vehicle." Once again, this may cost you more up front when making your purchase, but I believe that this is one of the best programs ever offered to potential used car buyers.

AutoSave Tip

Take advantage of your warranty. There are two things you should do. First, have the vehicle inspected by an independent mechanic right after you purchase it. Show him or her the warranty you have, and have all the items it covers checked out. This can prevent the hassles of a future breakdown. The second thing is to have the vehicle completely checked out just before the warranty ends. This can save you a tremendous amount of future expenses, especially because everything seems to go wrong after the warranty ends. Few items suddenly just go bad. Parts such as the transmission may take months to develop into a problem that you finally notice.

Summary

Although the purchase of a used vehicle will often offer you a lot more for the selling price, the overall cost of a used vehicle purchase often outweighs the benefits of buying new, especially when you consider the options of leasing or the overall costs of financing and/or maintenance. Not to say that purchasing a used vehicle cannot be a good value, but the "big picture" must be kept in mind. What new rules, then, should you have learned from this section?

1. Look beyond the selling price of a vehicle before you consider used. Remember to keep the "big picture" in mind.

2. If you buy used, make sure you have the vehicle checked by a reputable mechanic before you commit to the purchase.

---

3. Ask exactly what is covered by a warranty offered on a used vehicle, and remember that many late model vehicles may have the balance of a factory warranty, whether the seller has told you so or not.

4. "Certified" vehicles will almost always ensure a greater level of ownership satisfaction with your purchase.

5. If you consider the option of leasing a used vehicle, be sure to compare the cost to what it might be to lease a brand new one.

Chapter 8

After the deal is made

Changing your mind

Most reputable dealerships are very flexible about how they do business. You can usually change almost any aspect of the deal you have made as long as nothing has been done to alter the original vehicle you agreed to purchase. If the dealership has already applied a product such as rust-proofing or an alarm system, you may still be able to change vehicles, but you will most likely be held responsible for the cost of whatever changes have been made to the original vehicle.

If you have placed a factory order for a vehicle, changing your mind could be more of a problem. Again, the dealership cannot force you to take the vehicle, but you can be held responsible for a percentage of its cost. In many cases, if the vehicle you originally ordered is not something out of the ordinary, a dealership will usually just put that vehicle into its stock and not give you a hard time—assuming, of course, that you are still going to purchase another vehicle from that dealership.

AutoSave Tip

It is always a good idea to leave the smallest possible deposit when you have negotiated your deal. The more money of yours a dealership has, the stronger it will fight to keep it. The less you have paid, the lower your possible loss might be.

When it comes to canceling a deal, many consumers are confused about how the law works. I have known customers to call the day after a purchase, suffering from "buyer's remorse." They would attempt to explain that, under the law, a consumer has 72 hours to change his or her mind.

This is not always true. In most states, the 72-hour law only applies if a salesperson came to you and then you decided you didn't want to go through with the purchase. For example, the law would apply to door-to-door magazine and vacuum cleaner salespeople. With automobile purchases, however, you have come to the dealership and your contract is usually binding. By law, the dealership can refuse to refund your deposit. Be sure to check your own state's laws regarding sales contracts.

AutoSave Tip

You may be told that the dealership will not refund your deposit, but this rarely has to be the case. Continue to call the manager requesting your deposit back. He or she may simply get fed up with hearing from you and return your money. Another option is small claims court. Although you signed a contract, most courts are very *pro*-consumer and *anti*-car dealership. If you can show good cause for why you changed your mind, the judge may award your refund. In many cases, it doesn't even get that far. The time involved in going to court is often not worth it to the dealership. Once the dealership has received the papers notifying it of your pending court action, it will often just send your money back.

What if you're not satisfied?

Automobiles are machines, and even the very best ones can have problems. Although many people don't think so, car salespeople and managers are human, and they, too, can make mistakes. As with any problem, the way you handle problems with your vehicle will usually determine the results you get. Ranting, raving and making threats will rarely help your cause; it may, in fact, hurt it. By nature, we tend to cooperate better with calm people. Always stay calm.

Your complaint will usually be something the dealership has confronted before. The first thing to do is inquire if the dealership has a customer relations representative; better ones usually do. This person usually reports only to the owner of the dealership or to the next-in-charge. You can make the most of your time and effort by getting your complaint heard and handled by this person. If there is no customer relations representative, try the following:

Salesperson. If you have a problem with the salesperson, ask to see the general manager, not the sales manager. A salesperson is often only doing what the sales manager has told him or her to do. If you do not get the results you require, ask to speak with the owner. Employees may come and go, but the owner is usually a lot more concerned about his or her overall reputation.

Sales management. Again, look to speak with the general manager or owner. Contacting a dealership's district sales office usually won't do you much good. Car dealerships are franchises. They cannot be told how to conduct their business.

Service. Ask to speak with the service manager. Service managers are often sent to schools just to be trained in how to deal with the public. Do not attempt to speak with a service manager during the early morning or late afternoon hours. This is the busiest time and much of what you have to say will either be cut short or fall on deaf ears. If you are not satisfied with his or her response, once again, look to see if the dealership has a customer relations representative.

AutoSave Tip

Manufacturers have financial budgets designed specifically for customer relations. If you are not satisfied with any part of your vehicle, ask to see the district representative. The job of a manufacturer's customer relations department is to help keep up brand loyalty. I have seen members of this department pay for part or all of a problem that was nothing more than consumer abuse. This was done in the name of "customer relations."

If all else fails, this is usually the one area where the manufacturer's district office can be of help. It always has a customer relations department. Someone from the district office may look into your problem personally, or he or she may pressure the dealership to do so.

Try not to make threats. I have seen consumers threaten to picket a dealership, write letters to newspapers or politicians, drive through the showroom window and numerous other ill intents brought on by the heat of the moment. Again, you need to remain calm. People, by nature, always deal better when they are not threatened.

*Many of the threats consumers make really have no ef-
fect on a dealership. For example, a good portion of a newspaper's income comes from car dealership advertisements,
and few newspapers will print anything negative about
businesses that are helping them make a living. Also, a good
portion of the sales tax revenues for many states comes from
car sales, so government often turns the other way in response to complaints about car dealerships. Local consumer
reporting agencies will give you the best results. And if you
have purchased from a reputable dealership, your problems
will be taken care of.*

Becoming a more satisfied owner

Buying from the right dealership and choosing the right vehicle
are both important parts of being satisfied with your purchase. Properly maintaining your vehicle is another part. Every consumer who
ever bragged to me about putting tremendous amounts of mileage on
a vehicle or claimed they never had a problem with a vehicle had one
thing in common—they took good care of their vehicles. Automobiles
are not like appliances. You don't have them fixed only when they
break down. A regular program of maintenance, such as changing the
oil every 2,500 to 3,000 miles, can even help to make a vehicle with a
poor reliability rating a pleasure to own.

Choosing certain options discussed in Chapter 6, can also add to
your long-term enjoyment. Items such as extended warranties may
help provide a routine maintenance budget and help you avoid any
large unexpected expenses.

Summary

Once again, you should keep in mind that cars are just machines.
Getting yourself worked up over a problem is not going to do you or
the vehicle any good. Making up your mind that you will never purchase a particular brand again because you once had problems with it
is also not a good idea. Rarely does "100 percent satisfaction" exist.
You have to go with the odds. If you follow the odds and happen to fall
into the percentage that does have a problem, keep in mind that percentage always existed.

What you have learned

The purpose of this guide was not to teach you how to deal with all of the problems that it poses to you, but rather how to avoid them. You will be able to relate much of the information given to experiences that you've already had when shopping for a vehicle. If you follow the basic shopping guidelines that have been offered to you here, keeping the "big picture" in mind, you will avoid many of the problems described throughout this book. Remember, the best way to win at this particular game is by taking control of the situation and changing the rules in your favor. The following is a brief outline of the steps this guide has attempted to teach you:

First. Make a list of what you need and want from the vehicle you will eventually choose. This list should include all the options, such as two-door, four-door, five-passenger, six-passenger, air conditioning and so on. This list should also include all of your up-front decisions on extras, such as an extended warranty, alarm system and the like.

Second. Now that you know specifically what you want and need from your vehicle, you must establish your budget before you start to shop!

Third. Once you know exactly how much you can afford to spend, you should decide how you are going to spend it. This means whether you are going to pay cash, finance or lease and, if so, for what term. This doesn't mean you may not change your mind once you start to shop; incentive programs being offered by a manufacturer must also be a consideration. The point is to keep an open mind and always examine all of the alternatives.

Fourth. You should begin to research your options. Numerous automobile magazines and publications can offer in-depth information about areas such as reliability, complete make and model and breakdowns of available options, and many go so far as to list prices with them. When your book research is completed, you should have your choices narrowed down to no more than two or three vehicles for which you intend to shop.

Fifth. Now it is time to take a closer look at the vehicles you are considering. Unless you are very pressed for time, whom you intend to buy from is not yet important. You should be in the showrooms sitting in the vehicles, test driving them and possibly gaining incentive program information.

Sixth. By now, you should have narrowed your choices down to one or possibly two vehicles—no more than that. It is time to start doing your shopping. The first step should be to acquire dealer cost on your choice(s). You should always be negotiating from dealer cost up, not list price down.

Seventh. Now that you know what the dealership has paid for the vehicle(s) that you are considering, it is time to research dealerships. Regardless of the brand(s) you have chosen, odds are that at least two dealerships are conveniently located in your area. Follow the advice given in the section "Choosing the 'right' dealership" on page 46 in Chapter 2 and "Choosing the 'right' salesperson" on page 66 in Chapter 3.

Eighth. Now that you know what you want, how you are going to pay for it and from whom you are going to purchase it, your next step should be to call and make an appointment to see a salesperson. Tell the salesperson that you will be on time and that you expect him or her to be available to take care of you.

Ninth. Present the salesperson with your offer on the vehicle and any extras you have selected. Remember that anytime you are quoted a deal on a vehicle, that quote should be such that you could hand it over in cash and take the vehicle on the spot. Tell the salesperson how you have decided to pay for the vehicle and what you expect from your manner of payment. (This refers to items such as life and disability insurance with your loan, mileage on your lease and so on.)

When you are looking for a total delivered price, most salespeople are trained to tell you that they can't give you all of the information. For example, if you decided to purchase an extended warranty, the salesperson might tell you that his or her job is just to get you the price on the vehicle and that you can speak with someone else after the deal is made about the cost of the warranty you desire. This is playing by their rules, not yours! Your rules state that you only negotiate a complete selling price that includes everything you went shopping for!

Tenth. When the deal is made, it is time to pick the actual vehicle you are going to purchase. When this is done, be sure the serial number of the vehicle you have chosen is written on your sales order. If you are not purchasing from the dealer's stock, follow the information given in "Dealer 'locates' and 'factory orders'" on page 76 in Chapter 3.

Eleventh. Make an appointment to take delivery of your vehicle. If possible, the appointment should be during the day so you can better inspect the vehicle. When you arrive, do not sign any papers until you have inspected the vehicle and tested all of the options. This should include a test drive. Don't forget to check the amount of gas the vehicle has, and make sure any other items you may have purchased with the vehicle have been installed. Unless you really need to, don't take delivery of a vehicle until everything is exactly what you paid for.

Twelfth. Inspect all of the documents and make sure that you thoroughly understand them before you sign anything. Take all of the time you need and make sure the salesperson explains everything to you.

**Good luck with your purchase,
but we're not finished yet!**

---

1. Inform the dealer immediately about any problem(s) with the vehicle that you might have overlooked when you took delivery.
2. If you have purchased a used vehicle, be sure to follow the information in this guide about a mechanical check-out and making use of the warranty.
3. If you have chosen to lease your vehicle, be sure to use the information supplied in this guide about what to do before your lease is over.
4. Last, but not least, properly maintain your vehicle. Little can help with the reliability and overall satisfaction of your purchase as much as keeping up with a regular maintenance schedule.

If you follow this outline and you use the information that has been given in this guide, your purchase, and all of your future purchases, will be remembered as the "best deals" you ever made!

With any instructional guide, there are usually unanswered questions the reader still has. If there is anything I have not covered or you did not understand and you would like further information, I welcome your letters. Write to:

Kurt Allen Weiss
c/o Career Press, Inc.
3 Tice Road, P.O. Box 687
Franklin Lakes, NJ 07417

or e-mail Kurt directly at Gotadeal4u@aol.com

I hope you have found this guide informative. More so, I hope it will save you a lot of money. I am very interested in hearing from you. If this guide has helped you in any specific ways, please tell me about them. If you have any suggestions about how I might make it more informative, feel free to include them in your letter.

Write a letter to your governor...

...or even just me! Consumers have always complained about car salespeople. Surveys have shown that most complaints refer to a salesperson's lack of product knowledge or level of honesty. As of now, only a few states have attempted to do something about this. I believe every state should implement the following proposal.

With most important purchases we consider, such as a home or insurance, we turn to a licensed professional. With most problems we have requiring a doctor, a lawyer or even a plumber, we also turn to a licensed professional. Why, then, when we want to purchase a new car, don't we demand to deal with a licensed professional?

Car salespeople have the unique position of selling us one of the most expensive, most technical and most high-maintenance products that we will ever purchase, and they need no licensing or formal training to do so.

As I stated, some states have already done something about this problem. They have required the licensing of car salespeople. What would this license mean to you, the consumer?

Well, first of all, after spending more than 15 years in automobile sales myself, I can tell you it would immediately eliminate most of the unknowledgeable and dishonest salespeople. The first ones to go would mostly be the "fast talkers." The ones who relied on their mouths to sell, not their brains or their ears. They simply wouldn't take the time and effort to go through licensing or certification.

There is no question in my mind that, through the licensing and/ or certification of car salespeople, the majority of those who now make their living by "guesswork" or dishonesty would be eliminated. Imagine dealing with car salespeople who knew what they were talking about and actually tried to help you because if they didn't, they could lose their license to sell. Now that the bottom of the barrel has been eliminated, what else would licensing do for us?

Who do you turn to when you have a complaint about an unqualified or dishonest car salesperson? You can complain to his or her boss, but if the salesperson is making money, the boss usually just won't care. You can file a complaint with a local agency, such as the Better Business Bureau, but most of these agencies only handle complaints about the businesses themselves. Through licensing, we have some form of recourse. Just as drivers with too many points for traffic violations have their driver's licenses revoked, salespeople who receive too many complaints about them will have their licenses taken away.

I don't think it's a lot to ask such highly paid professionals as car salespeople that they become responsible to consumers. And I don't think it's a lot to ask that we, the consumers, simply stop complaining about car salespeople and do something about it. Cast your vote! Write to your governor and tell him or her that you are sick and tired of dealing with unprofessional and/or dishonest car salespeople. Tell him or her that you vote for the licensing and/or certification of car salespeople. If you don't want to write to your governor, then write to me. I will join your votes together in a letter of petition to help ensure that the powers that be hear your voice.

How to use the forms

The following forms are of my own design and are simply intended to be used as tools to help you organize your approach to the shopping experience. You may wish to make up your own forms, but the point is that you should be using something. Dealerships and salespeople count on consumers to go shopping for a vehicle unprepared. Some people may feel embarrassed about bringing a form with them to the showroom. I can only say that I would rather be embarrassed than taken advantage of!

Using the amortization tables

You should find the following tables easy to use. The top numbers show the length of a loan in months. The numbers on the left represent interest rates from 2 to 20 percent in 1/4 percent intervals. The point at which the length of the loan and the interest rate meet shows the monthly payment factor for every dollar that you finance.

For example, if you borrow $12,428.72 for 48 months at 9.25 percent interest, you would figure the monthly payment amount in the following way: 12,428.72 x .025004 = 310.77. The product is your monthly payment. The .025004 is the monthly payment factor, found where 48 months and 9.25 percent interest intersect.

Not all loans are amortized the same way. These tables are only meant to be guidelines, although their results are usually accurate.

Loan Amortization Tables
(without L, A & H insurance)

Number of Months

APR	(12)	(24)	(30)	(36)	(42)	(48)	(54)	(60)
2.00	.084239	.042540	.034201	.028643	.024672	.021695	.019380	.017528
2.25	.084352	.042650	.043311	.028752	.024782	.021804	.019489	.017637
2.50	.084466	.042760	.034421	.028861	.024891	.021914	.019599	.017747
2.75	.084580	.042871	.034530	.028971	.025001	.022024	.019709	.017858
3.00	.084694	.042981	.034641	.029081	.025111	.022134	.019820	.017969
3.25	.084808	.043092	.034751	.029192	.025222	.022245	.019931	.018080
3.50	.084922	.043203	.034861	.029302	.025332	.022356	.020042	.018192
3.75	.085036	.043314	.034972	.029413	.025443	.022467	.020154	.018304
4.00	.085150	.043425	.035083	.029524	.025555	.022579	.020266	.018417
4.25	.085264	.043536	.035194	.029635	.025666	.022691	.020378	.018530
4.50	.085379	.043648	.035306	.029747	.025778	.022803	.020491	.018643
4.75	.085493	.043760	.035418	.029859	.025890	.022916	.020605	.018757
5.00	.085607	.043871	.035529	.029971	.026003	.023029	.020718	.018871
5.25	.085722	.043983	.035641	.030083	.026116	.023143	.020832	.018986
5.50	.085837	.044096	.035754	.030196	.026229	.023256	.020947	.019101
5.75	.085952	.044208	.035866	.030309	.026342	.023371	.021062	.019217
6.00	.086066	.044321	.035979	.030422	.026456	.023485	.021177	.019333
6.25	.086181	.044433	.036092	.030535	.026570	.023600	.021292	.019449
6.50	.086296	.044546	.036205	.030649	.026685	.023715	.021408	.019566
6.75	.086412	.044659	.036318	.030763	.026799	.023830	.021525	.019683
7.00	.086527	.044773	.036432	.030877	.026914	.023946	.021642	.019801
7.25	.086642	.044886	.036546	.030992	.027029	.024062	.021759	.019919
7.50	.086757	.045000	.036660	.031106	.027145	.024179	.021876	.020038
7.75	.086873	.045113	.036774	.031221	.027261	.024296	.021994	.020157
8.00	.086988	.045227	.036888	.031336	.027377	.024413	.022112	.020276
8.25	.087104	.045341	.037003	.031452	.027493	.024530	.022231	.020396
8.50	.087220	.045456	.037118	.031568	.027610	.024648	.022350	.020517
8.75	.087336	.045570	.037233	.031684	.027727	.024767	.022470	.020637
9.00	.087451	.045685	.037348	.031800	.027845	.024885	.022589	.020758
9.25	.087567	.045800	.037464	.031916	.027962	.025004	.022710	.020880
9.50	.087684	.045914	.037579	.032033	.028080	.025123	.022830	.021002
9.75	.087800	.046030	.037695	.032150	.028198	.025243	.022951	.021124

Loan Amortization Tables
(cont.)

Number of Months

APR	(12)	(24)	(30)	(36)	(42)	(48)	(54)	(60)
10.00	.087916	.046145	.037811	.032267	.028317	.025363	.023072	.021247
10.25	.088032	.046260	.037928	.032385	.028436	.025483	.023194	.021370
10.50	.088149	.046376	.038044	.032502	.028555	.025603	.023316	.021494
10.75	.088265	.046492	.038161	.032620	.028674	.025724	.023439	.021618
11.00	.088382	.046608	.038278	.032739	.028794	.025846	.023561	.021742
11.25	.088498	.046724	.038395	.032857	.028914	.025967	.023685	.021867
11.50	.088615	.046840	.038513	.032976	.029034	.026089	.023808	.021993
11.75	.088732	.046957	.038630	.033095	.029155	.026211	.023932	.022118
12.00	.088849	.047073	.038748	.033214	.029276	.026334	.024057	.022244
12.25	.088966	.047190	.038866	.033334	.029397	.026457	.024181	.022371
12.50	.089083	.047307	.038984	.033454	.029518	.026580	.024306	.022498
12.75	.089200	.047424	.039103	.033574	.029640	.026704	.024432	.022625
13.00	.089317	.047542	.039222	.033694	.029762	.026827	.024558	.022753
13.25	.089435	.047659	.039340	.033814	.029884	.026952	.024684	.022881
13.50	.089552	.047777	.039460	.033935	.030007	.027076	.024810	.023010
13.75	.089670	.047895	.039579	.034056	.030130	.027201	.024937	.023139
14.00	.089787	.048013	.039698	.034178	.030253	.027326	.025065	.023268
14.25	.089905	.048131	.039818	.034299	.030377	.027452	.025192	.023398
14.50	.090023	.048249	.039938	.034421	.030501	.027578	.025320	.023528
14.75	.090140	.048368	.040058	.034543	.030625	.027704	.025449	.023659
15.00	.090258	.048487	.040179	.034665	.030749	.027831	.025578	.023790
15.25	.090376	.048606	.040299	.034788	.030874	.027958	.025707	.023921
15.50	.090494	.048725	.040420	.034911	.030999	.028085	.025836	.024053
15.75	.090613	.048844	.040541	.035034	.031124	.028212	.025966	.024185
16.00	.090731	.048963	.040662	.035157	.031250	.028340	.026096	.024318
16.25	.090849	.049083	.040783	.035281	.031375	.028468	.026227	.024451
16.50	.090968	.049202	.040905	.035404	.031501	.028597	.026358	.024585
16.75	.091086	.049322	.041027	.035528	.031628	.028726	.026489	.024718
17.00	.091205	.049442	.041149	.035653	.031755	.028803	.026568	.024799
17.25	.091323	.049562	.041271	.035777	.031882	.028985	.026753	.024987
17.50	.091442	.049683	.041394	.035902	.032009	.029114	.026885	.025122
17.75	.091561	.049803	.041516	.036027	.032136	.029245	.027018	.025258
18.00	.091680	.049924	.041639	.036152	.032264	.029375	.027151	.025393
18.25	.091799	.050045	.041762	.036278	.032392	.029506	.027285	.025530
18.50	.091918	.050166	.041886	.036404	.032521	.029637	.027419	.025666
18.75	.092037	.050287	.042009	.036530	.032650	.029768	.027553	.025803
19.00	.092157	.050409	.042133	.036656	.032778	.029900	.027687	.025941
19.25	.092276	.050530	.042257	.036783	.032908	.030032	.027822	.026078
19.50	.092395	.050652	.042381	.036909	.033037	.030165	.027958	.026216
19.75	.092515	.050774	.042505	.037036	.033167	.030297	.028093	.026355
20.00	.092635	.050896	.042630	.037164	.033297	.030430	.028229	.026494

Using the brand comparison form

The form on page 179 is designed to help you choose a particular vehicle. As discussed in "Comparing brands" on page 31 in Chapter 2, this form should be used when you initially go to the dealership just to look at, sit in and test drive the choices you have made so far.

1. Make note of the day you saw the vehicle and enter any appointment you make to come back.
2. List the make, model and designation of the vehicle. Example: Ford Taurus GL.
3. List pertinent information on the dealership and salesperson.
4. For reference only, note the list price of the vehicle you looked at, as well as any sale price you are aware of.
5. Inquire about incentive programs that may currently be in effect.
6. Circle the major options the vehicle has and then list any extras:

A/T = Automatic Transmission	A/C = Air Conditioning	P/S = Power Steering
Brakes D = Disk Front/Rear	ABS = Antilock Brake	ST = Stereo
Cass = Cassette	CD = Compact Disc	RD = Rear Defroster
TW = Tilt Wheel	C/C = Cruise Control	PW = Power Windows
S/R = Sun Roof - Manual or Pwr	PD = Pwr Door Lcks	CPL = Child Proof Lcks
Lthr = Leather	# Pass = Passenger Capacity	Mirrors = Remote/Power

7. Next, fill in engine specifications:

Cyls = Cylinders	Turbo = Turbo Charged Engine	Tq = Torque
Mpg = Miles per gallon	C, H = City and Highway	HP = Horse Power
E.F.I. = Electronic Fuel Injection		

8. Fill in what the standard warranty is and inquire about the price of an extended warranty that fits your driving needs.
9. Rate your test drive:

   E = Excellent   G = Good   F = Fair   P = Poor
10. Next, list any other items that you feel are good points or drawbacks of the vehicle.

You will be able to use some of the vehicle information, along with the impressions you got of the dealership or salesperson, to start filling in your "shopping list."

Brand Comparison Form

Date Seen:_____ Appointment Date:_____ Time:_____

Make:_____ Model:_____ Designation:_____

Dealer:_____ Address:_____

Town:_____ Phone:_____ Hours:_____

Sales Rep:_____ Referred By:_____

List Price:$_____ Sale Price (If Known):$_____

Fin/Lease Programs: (%_____Mths_____) (%_____Mths_____) (%_____Mths_____)

Rebate Incentive: $_____ Good With Finance [Y] [N] Good Until_____

Major Opts: [A/T] [A/C] [PS] [BRAKES (D)-(F) (R) - (ABS)] [ST-CASS-CD] [RD] [TW] [C/C] [S/R - M - P] [CPSL] [PW] [PD] [# PASS-____] [Mirrors] [Lthr]

Extra's:_____

_____

Engine: Cyls____Liters____HP_____Tq_____MPG C-____H-____ E.F.I. [Y][N] Turbo [Y][N]

StdWarranty:Full-Yrs_____Miles_____PwrTrain-Yrs_____Miles_____

Extended Cost $_____Yrs_____Miles_____Type_____

Test Drive - [Y] [N]   Comfort - [E] [G] [F] [P]   Ride/Handling - [E] [G] [F] [P]

Good   Points:_____

_____

_____

Draw-backs :_____

_____

_____

Notes:

Using the shopping list

By using the information you got from the brand comparison form and your own personal research, you should be able to start making your shopping list. Use the one I've supplied on page 182. You will fill out most of it when you are at the dealership. Intentionally, there's room for only two dealerships. If you have followed what this guide has attempted to teach you, that will be enough.

1. Start with filling in the make, model and designation of the vehicle you are going to shop.

2. Now view the average city and highway mileage and estimate the one figure that would be your average, based on how and where you drive. Figure out how many miles a month you drive and divide that by the average m.p.g. you listed. Multiply the result by your local average per-gallon fuel costs, and fill in how much a month in fuel that vehicle will cost you.

3. Fill in the maximum down payment and monthly payment you have selected. This information is from the budget form on page 39.

4. Fill in current incentive programs you might have learned of when you did your brand comparison shopping.

5. Circle the decisions you have made regarding L, A & H and an extended warranty. If you have decided on a warranty, fill in the time that you plan to keep your vehicle, along with the mileage you expect to put on it. This will help you decide on the right warranty.

6. Fill in the options and/or option package number that you have chosen.

7. Under the heading "Other," fill in any after-sell products you want, such as an extended warranty, alarm and so forth.

8. Fill in the dealership information, including information about loaner cars or rental car availability, and list the dealership's service hours.

9. If you are going to shop more than one dealership, fill in the M.S.R.P. of the vehicle. This is very important for comparison shopping. Not all dealerships stock their vehicles exactly the same. Unless the M.S.R.P. matches, you may need to take a closer look at what you are comparing. Dealer cost can be filled in either from a service or publication that you bought or by using the amount from an actual dealer invoice. Next, fill in your negotiated price.

10. Continue listing the after-sell options you selected with their cost to you.

11. Fill in the package number of the vehicle you negotiated, as well as any individual option extras. This second listing is a double-check for shopping between dealerships.

12. Finally, fill in the *complete delivered price,* as if you were going to hand over the cash and take the vehicle on the spot.

13. The shopping list is not just designed for your dealership-to-dealership comparative shopping. It is also designed to keep the decisions you should have made before you started shopping in front of you.

Have I Got a Deal for You!

Shopping List

Make: _____ Model: _____ Designation: _____

MPG Avg: _____ Miles per Mth: _____ Mthly Fuel Cost: _____

Maximum Down-Payment _____ Maximum Mthly Budget _____

Current Incentives _____ Good Till: _____

L, A&H - [Y] [N]   Extended Warranty - [Y] [N]   Term - Yrs _____ Miles _____

Options: _____ , _____ , _____ , _____

_____ , _____ , _____ , _____

Other : _____ , _____ , _____ , _____

(Dealer 1)
Name: _____ Phone: _____ Salesman: _____

Location: _____ Appointment: _____

Loaner Cars [Y] [N]   Rentals [Y] [N] Service Hours: _____

M.S.R.P.: $ _____ Cost?: $ _____ Selling Price:$ _____

After-Sell 1. _____ $ _____ 2. _____ $ _____

3. _____ $ _____ 4. _____ $ _____

Pkg #: _____ Extra's: _____ , _____ , _____

_____ , _____ , _____ , _____ , _____

Total Delivered Price (taxes, after-sell, M.V., etc) $ _____

(Dealer 2)
Name: _____ Phone: _____ Salesman: _____

Location: _____ Appointment: _____

Loaner Cars [Y] [N]   Rentals [Y] [N]   Service Hours: _____

M.S.R.P.: $ _____ Cost?: $ _____ Selling Price: $ _____

After-Sell 1. _____ $ _____ 2. _____ $ _____

3. _____ $ _____ 4. _____ $ _____

Pkg #: _____ Extra's: _____ , _____ , _____

_____ , _____ , _____ , _____ , _____

Total Delivered Price (taxes, after-sell, M.V., etc) $ _____

Commonly used words and phrases

A.C.V. (Actual Cash Value). Refers to the actual, not inflated, value that a dealership considers a customer's trade to be worth.

Add-on label. Also referred to as a "gaff sticker," it is a label that a dealership puts on a vehicle in addition to the manufacturer's sticker. It is usually comprised of "protection packages" or "market availability fees." Its purpose is to raise the retail price of the vehicle in an attempt to increase profit levels.

After-market. Nonfactory options or accessories added to a vehicle by either the dealership or an outside company.

After-sell. The sale of nonoriginal options or products in addition to the vehicle itself.

Allocation or allotment. A term most commonly used among import dealerships, it refers to the availability of a particular product or product line. Most vehicles that have import restrictions are allocated to the dealership based on its volume of sales. Other vehicles may be allocated because of production availability or any reason causing a short supply.

Allowance. Refers to an inflated value that a dealership will offer a customer for his or her trade-in. For example, a discount on the selling price of a new vehicle may be wrapped into the amount the customer is quoted for his or her trade-in, thus inflating the value of the trade-in. Refer to **A.C.V.**

APR. Annual Percentage Rate or Actual Percentage Rate.

"As-is." Referring to a used vehicle, it is a vehicle that is offered without any form of guarantee or warranty.

Back-end. The profit the dealership makes on anything other than the vehicle itself. This profit generally includes finance and after-sell income.

Bird dog and **bird dog fee.** A "bird dog" refers business to a dealership or salesperson, and "bird dog fee" is the money he or she receives for doing so.

Blue Book. The *Kelly Blue Book* is one of numerous publications that offers a factory equipment price list based on "list" and "cost" prices of vehicles, including their projected future values.

(The) Box. The box is the area (office) in which the business manager, also referred to as the finance manager, works. When a customer is sent to "the box," it generally means the back-end sales practice is about to begin.

Bump. This is when the dealership or salesperson has been able to increase the price or payment that a customer originally agreed upon.

Bureau. Refers to a credit reporting agency. A dealership will have a bureau report run to qualify a customer's credit.

Buried. Referring to a customer as "buried" usually means that he or she owes more on his or her trade than it is worth. Salespeople sometimes use the phrase "I buried that customer," meaning that they made so much profit that it will be difficult for the customer to ever get rid of the vehicle until it is completely paid for. Also referred to as "upside down."

Buyer's order. The sales form used to write up a customer's purchase. Also known as a sales contract or purchase order.

Cap cost. A lease term that refers to the actual amount being financed (leased); it is meant to represent "selling price."

Cap reduction. A down payment or discount on a vehicle being leased. A trade-in is often used as a cap reduction.

Certificate of Origin (C of O). The original title to the vehicle showing where it originated and if it has ever been previously titled.

Charge-off. Credit that has been deemed uncollectible by the lender and listed as such on a customer's credit report.

Closer. The person or persons used to close a deal when the original salesperson is unsuccessful. Often introduced as a manager, another salesperson is often used as a closer.

Dealer installed. Any equipment, original or after-market, that is installed on the vehicle by dealerships themselves.

Dealer swap. The exchanging of vehicles between dealerships; what usually transpires with a dealer locate.

Debt to income ratio. A formula used by banks to determine whether or not a consumer can afford the loan for which he or she applied. Without taking other outstanding debts into consideration, a general rule is that an auto loan should not exceed one week's gross income.

Demo (demonstrator). A vehicle that is driven "untitled," usually by a dealership employee.

Destination charges. The amount charged by the manufacturer to ship the vehicle from the factory to the dealership or, in the case of imports, from the port to the dealership. Also referred to as "freight."

Detail. What a dealership generally does to a used vehicle. This is the process of thoroughly cleaning it, inside and out, to make it presentable for sale.

F & I. Stands for finance and insurance; usually refers to the department where the "business manager" works.

Fleet rebate. A manufacturer to business rebate; a special rebate program for businesses that buy in volume each year. Most of these programs require the business to purchase a minimum of five to 10 vehicles a year from the manufacturer. They do not always have to be of the same brand. Usually in lieu of any normal consumer programs in effect.

Front end. Refers to the amount of dealer profit on the sale of the vehicle itself above dealer invoice.

Gray market. Refers to a vehicle that has been brought into the United States and has bypassed the D.O.T. (Department of Transportation) regulations. These vehicles are usually not equipped to pass U.S. emissions standards, and manufacturers usually do not back their warranties.

Gross. The amount of profit made on a deal.

High-ball. Similar to low-ball, this tactic is generally used with trade-ins. It is when a customer is quoted a higher value for his or her trade-in than the dealership actually intends to give.

Hold-back. A percentage of each vehicle that is given back to the dealership by the manufacturer. It represents a profit area that is considered "under invoice" income. This profit area is rarely used as a part of dealership to consumer negotiations.

Home run. When a higher-than-usual profit is made.

In-house. The word "house" refers to the dealership. The phrase "in-house" refers to something the dealership is doing on its own. Some after-market products are installed "in-house." Some dealerships offer "in-house" financing.

Invoice. The dollar amount on the dealership's invoice from the manufacturer representing a dealership's cost, excluding hold-back profit. (Hold-back profit is shown on a dealership's invoice.)

L, A & H. Life, accident and health insurance. This is a policy on the borrower of a loan, which insures his or her monthly or entire loan payment in the event of death, injury or illness.

Lemon laws. Consumer protection laws governed by each state individually, giving the consumer a means of recourse should a vehicle have unusual or continual problems. It is designed to allow the consumer to return a vehicle that qualifies under the laws' guidelines.

Load-up. See **Packing** or **packing-in**.

Locates. The process of locating a vehicle in the inventory of another dealership; an alternative to factory orders or buying "out-of-stock."

Locator. The computer program that is used by dealerships to "locate" a vehicle.

Low-ball. The practice of "quoting" a price that is lower than the dealership intends to honor. This technique can be used with locates, factory orders, interest rates, monthly payments or with any figure the dealership has the opportunity to change.

Market value. The value for which a vehicle can be retailed in a given geographic area.

Monroney label. The actual manufacturer's window sticker that will show the price, equipment and fuel economy of a new vehicle. It is named for the congressman who instituted its use.

M.S.R.P. Manufacturer's Suggested Retail Price.

M.V. Short for "motor vehicle," it is a term used in auto sales to represent a customer's registration and title fees. It may be quoted to the customer inclusive of a documentary fee.

N.A.D.A. National Automobile Dealers Association. It offers a periodic publication that provides a guideline for the retail, wholesale and loan value of a vehicle.

Negative equity. Refers to the amount by which a vehicle is worth less than a consumer still owes on it.

Nonrecourse. Refers to a dealership whose arrangement with its "financing" sources is such that the dealership is relieved of any responsibility for its customers' auto loans. Other than supplying background information on the applicant, this kind of dealership relies solely on the loan application decisions the bank makes. (See **Recourse.**)

Odometer statement. A legal document required by most states to be completed by both the dealership and the consumer, verifying the mileage of a vehicle.

Old car. Refers to a vehicle still in dealership inventory from a previous price level. Although manufacturers may have several price increases during a model year, once a vehicle receives a Monroney label, its individual price cannot be changed.

Over the curb. After all paperwork is completed and the vehicle is paid for in one manner or another, the vehicle becomes the legal possession of the buyer when it has been driven off the lot, or "over the curb."

Pack. A level of profit on new and used vehicles for which a dealership does not pay its salespeople commission.

Packing or **packing-in.** Refers to profits or products that are added to a deal or to the vehicle itself. These profits are often added without the customer's knowledge. An example would be the dealership "packing" profit into a lease-end purchase option or adding life, accident and health insurance to a loan without informing the customer.

P.D.I. Stands for predelivery inspection; also referred to as "prep." A vehicle is supposed to have its fluid levels, tire pressure, running condition and so on checked out before the consumer takes delivery of it. Although most manufacturers pay a fee to their dealerships to do this inspection, many dealerships do not with the intent of keeping this money as extra profit.

Penciled. Usually done by sales management with a red pen or marker, a customer's offer is crossed out, or "penciled," and the salesperson is sent back to try to get more money.

PEP. Popular Equipment Package or Preferred Equipment Package. This refers to grouping options together, a concept by which most vehicles are sold today.

Pop top. Refers to a sunroof that is manually removed or opened.

Port installed. When an import arrives at its U.S. destination (the port), extra options are often installed to raise its suggested retail price and offer the dealership a greater opportunity for profit. In addition, other items, such as air conditioners, are often port installed. This practice is used to avoid excess U.S. import tax. By shipping the air conditioner as a part, it is not subject to the taxes that would be levied on it if it were already on the vehicle, adding to that vehicle's cost.

Positive equity. The amount by which a vehicle is worth more than what is owed on it.

Power of attorney. A legal document authorizing someone to act on another's behalf. If a customer owes money on a trade-in, a dealership will have the customer sign a limited power of attorney giving the dealership the authority to pay off the customer's loan.

Protection package. A grouping of after-market products, such as combining rust-proofing with undercoating to create a "rust protection package."

Purchase option. A part of a lease contract giving the lessee the option to purchase the vehicle at the end of the lease.

Qualifying. When a salesperson asks a customer questions to gain "insight" into his or her readiness to purchase a vehicle and/or into his or her credit stability.

R.D.R. Retail Delivery Report. The paperwork that is completed by the dealership to report a vehicle as delivered. R.D.R.'s are often the foundation of an import dealership's allocation.

Recourse. Refers to a dealership whose arrangement with its "financing" sources is such that the dealership is responsible for its customers' auto loans. In addition to supplying the bank with customers' loan applications, this kind of dealership can take a gamble on its customers and make loan approval decisions on its own.

Residual value. The actual dollar value of a vehicle deferred to the end of the lease. It is used with cap cost to determine a customer's monthly lease payments. It is not necessarily the same amount as the "purchase option."

Soft. Refers to a model of vehicle that has generated little interest to consumers. A new or used vehicle can be soft.

Spot delivery. Refers to allowing a customer to take delivery of his or her vehicle at the same time the deal has been concluded. Some dealerships will run a credit report while negotiating with a customer. If the customer looks creditworthy, the dealership will allow him or her to take possession of the vehicle on the spot.

Sticker or **sticker price.** Refers to the Monroney label (window sticker) on a new vehicle with its M.S.R.P. (Manufacturer's Suggested Retail Price).

Stips. The conditions by which a bank is willing to approve a loan.

Street value. The retail value of a vehicle; not related to trade-in or wholesale value. Basically, the same as retail "market value."

Tag. Another term for "license plate."

Tissue. Another term for "dealer invoice."

T.O. When a salesperson cannot close a deal, he "T.O.'s" (turns it over) to another salesperson or manager.

Upside down. This means that a customer currently owes more on his or her vehicle than it is worth. Refer to **Buried**.

V.I.N. Vehicle Identification Number; also referred to as "serial number." It is found on the dashboard on the driver's side and is viewed through the outside of the windshield.

What if...? Would you...? "What if I could get it to you for this price?" and "Would you buy it now?" are the most common questions asked by a salesperson who is low-balling a customer. They seem to be questions that consumers never remember hearing—they only hear an offer being made. These questions can also be used as part of "qualifying" a customer's readiness to make a purchase decision.

Wheels. Refers to alloy or wire wheels, instead of standard hubcaps.

Wholesaler. A business or individual who buys used vehicles from one dealership to sell to another. Sometimes wholesalers make purchases for their own retail outlets.

Index